THE CLASS ST[RUGGLES]

IN FRA[NCE]

(1848-1850)

BY

KARL MARX

INTERNATIONAL PUBLISHERS

NEW YORK

This Printing, 1976

Library of Congress Catalog Card Number: 64-19792

ISBN: 0-7178-0030-x

MANUFACTURED IN THE UNITED STATES OF AMERICA

EDITOR'S NOTE

The present edition of this volume is a new translation. It contains the complete and accurate text of Engels' introduction written only a few months before his death. The passages omitted by the publishers of the original German edition are printed in italics and put in square brackets. An explanation of the reasons for the omissions will be found on page 151.

CONTENTS

INTRODUCTION [1]

By FREDERICK ENGELS

This newly republished work was Marx's first attempt, with the aid of his materialist conception, to explain a section of contemporary history from the given economic situation. In *The Communist Manifesto,* the theory was applied in broad outline to the whole of modern history, while in the articles by Marx and myself in the *Neue Rheinische Zeitung,* it was constantly used to interpret political events of the day. Here, on the other hand, the question was to demonstrate the inner causal connection in the course of a development which extended over some years, a development as critical, for the whole of Europe, as it was typical; that is, in accordance with the conception of the author, to trace political events back to the effects of what are, in the last resort, economic causes.

In judging the events and series of events of day-to-day history, it will never be possible for anyone to go right back to the final economic causes. Even today, when the specialized technical press provides such rich materials, in England itself it still remains impossible to follow day by day the movement of industry and trade in the world market and the changes which take place in the methods of production, in such a way as to be able to draw the general conclusion, at any point of time, from these very complicated and ever changing factors; of these factors, the most important, into the bargain, generally operate a long time in secret before they suddenly and violently make themselves felt on the surface. A clear survey of the economic history of a given period is never contemporaneous; it can only be gained subsequently, after collecting and sifting of the material has taken place. Statistics are a necessary help here, and they always lag behind. For this reason, it is only too often necessary, in the

9

current history of the time, to treat the most decisive factor as constant, to treat the economic situation existing at the beginning of the period concerned as given and unalterable for the whole period, or else to take notice only of such changes in this situation as themselves arise out of events clearly before us, and as, therefore, can likewise be clearly seen. Hence, the materialist method has here often to limit itself to tracing political conflicts back to the struggles between the interests of the social classes and fractions of classes encountered as the result of economic development, and to show the particular political parties as the more or less adequate political expression of these same classes and fractions of classes.

It is self-evident that this unavoidable neglect of contemporaneous changes in the economic situation, of the very basis of all the proceedings subject to examination, must be a source of error. But all the conditions of a comprehensive presentation of the history of the day unavoidably imply sources of error—which, however, keeps nobody from writing contemporary history.

When Marx undertook this work, the sources of error mentioned were, to a still greater degree, impossible to avoid. It was quite impossible during the period of the Revolution of 1848-49 to follow the economic transformations which were being consummated at the same time, or even to keep a general view of them. It was just the same during the first months of exile in London, in the autumn and winter of 1849-50. But that was just the time when Marx began this work. And in spite of these unfavorable circumstances, his exact knowledge both of the economic situation in France and of the political history of that country since the February Revolution, made it possible for him to give a picture of events which laid bare their inner connections in a way never attained since, and which later brilliantly withstood the double test instituted by Marx himself.

The first test resulted from the fact that after the spring of 1850 Marx once again found leisure for economic studies, and first of all took up the economic history of the last ten years. In this study, what he had earlier deduced, half *a priori*, from defective material, was made absolutely clear to him by the facts themselves, namely, that the world trade crisis of 1847 had been the true mother of the February and March Revolutions [2] and that the industrial prosperity which had been returning gradually since the middle of 1848, and which attained full bloom in 1849 and 1850, was the revivifying force of the newly strengthened European reaction. That was decisive. Whereas in the three first articles (which appeared in the January, February and March number of the *N. Rh. Z.*,* *politisch-ökonomische Revue*, Hamburg, 1850) there was still the expectation of an imminent new upsurge of revolutionary energy, the historical review written by Marx and myself for the last number, which was published in the autumn of 1850 (a double number, May to October), breaks once and for all with these illusions: "A new revolution is only possible as a result of a new crisis. It is just as certain, however, as this." But that was the only essential change which had to be made. There was absolutely nothing to alter in the interpretation of events given in the earlier chapters, or in the causal connections established therein, as the continuation of the narrative from March 10, up to the autumn of 1850 in the review in question, proves. I have therefore included this continuation as the fourth article in the present new edition.

The second test was even more severe. Immediately after Louis Bonaparte's *coup d'état* of December 2, 1851, Marx worked out anew the history of France from February 1848, up to this event, which concluded the revolutionary period for the time being. (*The Eighteenth Brumaire of Louis Bonaparte.* Third edition, Meissner, Hamburg, 1885.) In this brochure the period which we had depicted in our present publication is again dealt with, although more briefly. Compare this second production, written in the light of decisive events which happened over a year later, with our present publication, and it will be found that the author had very little to change.

The thing which still gives this work of ours a quite special significance is that, for the first time, it expresses the formula in which, by common agreement, the workers' parties of all countries in the world briefly summarize their demand for eco-

* *Neue Rheinische Zeitung.*

nomic reconstruction: the appropriation by society of the mean
of production. In the second chapter, in connection with the
"right to work," which is characterized as "the first clumsy
formula wherein the revolutionary aspirations of the proletariat
are summarized," it is said: "But behind the right to work stands
the power over capital; behind the power over capital, the appropriation of the means of production, their subjection to the
associated working class and, therefore, the abolition of wage
labor as well as of capital and of their mutual relationships."
Thus, here, for the first time, the proposition is formulated by
which modern working class socialism is equally sharply differentiated both from all the different shades of feudal, bourgeois,
petty-bourgeois, etc., socialism [3] and also from the confused
community of goods of utopian and spontaneous worker-
communism. If, later, Marx extended the formula to appropriation of the means of exchange also, this extension, which, in
any case, was self-evident after *The Communist Manifesto*, only
expressed a corollary to the main proposition. A few wiseacres
in England have of late added that the "means of distribution"
should also be handed over to society. It would be difficult for
these gentlemen to say what these economic means of distribution are, as distinct from the means of production and exchange;
unless political means of distribution are meant, taxes, poor
relief, including the *Sachsenwald* [4] and other endowments. But,
first, these are means of distribution now already in collective
possession, either of the state or of the commune, and, secondly,
it is precisely these we wish to abolish.

When the February Revolution broke out, we all of us, as
far as our conception of the conditions and the course of revolutionary movements was concerned, were under the spell of
previous historical experience, namely, that of France. It was,
indeed, the latter which had dominated the whole of European
history since 1789, and from which now once again the signal
had gone forth for general revolutionary change. It was therefore natural and unavoidable that our conceptions of the nature
and the path of the "social" revolution proclaimed in Paris in
February 1848, of the revolution of the proletariat, were

strongly colored by memories of the models of 1789-1830. Moreover, when the Paris upheaval found its echo in the victorious insurrections in Vienna, Milan and Berlin; when the whole of Europe right up to the Russian frontier was swept into the movement; when in Paris the first great battle for power between the proletariat and the bourgeoisie was joined; when the very victory of their class so shook the bourgeoisie of all countries that they fled back into the arms of the monarchist-feudal reaction which had just been overthrown—for us under the circumstances of the time, there could be no doubt that the great decisive struggle had broken out, that it would have to be fought out in a single, long and changeful period of revolution, but that it could only end with the final victory of the proletariat.

After the defeats of 1849 we in no way shared the illusions of the vulgar democracy grouped around the would-be provisional governments *in partibus*.* This vulgar democracy reckoned on a speedy and finally decisive victory of the "people" over the "usurpers"; we looked to a long struggle, after the removal of the "usurpers," between the antagonistic elements concealed within this "people" itself. Vulgar democracy expected a renewed outbreak from day to day; we declared as early as autumn 1850 that at least the first chapter of the revolutionary period was closed and that nothing further was to be expected until the outbreak of a new world crisis. For this reason we were excommunicated, as traitors to the revolution, by the very people who later, almost without exception, have made their peace with Bismarck—so far as Bismarck found them worth the trouble.

But we, too, have been shown to have been wrong by history, which has revealed our point of view of that time to have been an illusion. It has done even more: it has not merely destroyed our error of that time; it had also completely transformed the conditions under which the proletariat has to fight. The mode of struggle of 1848 is today obsolete from every point of view, and this is a point which deserves closer examination on the present occasion.

* *In partibus* (*infidelium*)—in the midst of the infidels, and so government that exists only on paper.

All revolutions up to the present day have resulted in the displacement of one definite class rule by another; all ruling classes up till now have been only minorities as against the ruled mass of the people. A ruling minority was thus overthrown; another minority seized the helm of state and remodeled the state apparatus in accordance with its own interests. This was on every occasion the minority group, able and called to rule by the degree of economic development, and just for that reason, and only for that reason, it happened that the ruled majority either participated in the revolution on the side of the former or else passively acquiesced in it. But if we disregard the concrete content of each occasion, the common form of all these revolutions was that they were minority revolutions. Even where the majority took part, it did so—whether wittingly or not—only in the service of a minority; but because of this, or simply because of the passive, unresisting attitude of the majority, this minority acquired the appearance of being the representative of the whole people.

As a rule, after the first great success, the victorious minority became divided; one half was pleased with what had been gained, the other wanted to go still further, and put forward new demands, which, to a certain extent at least, were also in the real or apparent interests of the great mass of the people. In individual cases these more radical demands were realized, but often only for the moment; the more moderate party again gained the upper hand, and what had eventually been won was wholly or partly lost again; the vanquished shrieked of treachery, or ascribed their defeat to accident. But in truth the position was mainly this: the achievements of the first victory were only safeguarded by the second victory of the more radical party; this having been attained, and, with it, what was necessary for the moment, the radicals and their achievements vanished once more from the stage.

All revolutions of modern times, beginning with the great English revolution of the seventeenth century, showed these features, which appeared inseparable from every revolutionary struggle. They appeared applicable, also, to the struggles of the proletariat for its emancipation; all the more applicable, since in 1848 there were few people who had any idea at all of the direction in which this emancipation was to be sought. The proletarian masses themselves, even in Paris, after the victory, were still absolutely in the dark as to the path to be taken. And yet the movement was there, instinctive, spontaneous, irrepressible. Was not this just the situation in which a revolution had to succeed, led certainly by a minority, but this time not in the interests of the minority, but in the real interests of the majority? If, in all the longer revolutionary periods, it was so easy to win the great masses of the people by the merely plausible and delusive views of the minorities thrusting themselves forward, how could they be less susceptible to ideas which were the truest reflex of their economic position, which were nothing but the clear, comprehensible expression of their needs, of needs not yet understood by themselves, but only vaguely felt? To be sure, this revolutionary mood of the masses had almost always, and usually very speedily, given way to lassitude or even to a revulsion to its opposite, so soon as illusion evaporated and disappointment set in. But here it was not a question of delusive views, but of giving effect to the very special interests of the great majority itself, interests, which at that time were certainly by no means clear to this great majority, but which must soon enough become clear in the course of giving practical effect to them, by their convincing obviousness. And if now, as Marx showed in the third article, in the spring of 1850, the development of the bourgeois republic that had arisen out of the "social" revolution of 1848 had concentrated the real power in the hands of the big bourgeoisie—monarchistically inclined as it was—and, on the other hand, had grouped all the other social classes, peasants as well as petty bourgeoisie, round the proletariat, so that, during and after the common victory, not they, but the proletariat grown wise by experience, must become the decisive factor—was there not every prospect here of turning the revolution of the minority into the revolution of the majority?

History has proved us, and all who thought like us, wrong. It has made it clear that the state of economic development on the

Continent at that time was not, by a long way, ripe for the removal of capitalist production; it has proved this by the economic revolution which, since 1848, has seized the whole of the Continent, has really caused big industry for the first time to take root in France, Austria, Hungary, Poland and, recently, in Russia, while it has made Germany positively an industrial country of the first rank—all on a capitalist basis, which in the year 1848, therefore, still had great capacity for expansion. But it is just this industrial revolution which has everywhere for the first time produced clarity in the class relationships, which has removed a number of transition forms handed down from the manufacturing period and in Eastern Europe even from guild handicraft, and has created a genuine bourgeoisie and a genuine large-scale industrial proletariat and pushed them into the foreground of social development. But owing to this, the struggle of these two great classes, which, apart from England, existed in 1848 only in Paris and, at the most, a few big industrial centers, has been spread over the whole of Europe and has reached an intensity such as was unthinkable in 1848. At that time the many obscure evangels of the sects, with their panaceas; today the one generally recognized, transparently clear theory of Marx, sharply formulating the final aims of the struggle. At that time the masses, sundered and differing according to locality and nationality, linked only by the feeling of common suffering, undeveloped, tossed to and fro in their perplexity from enthusiasm to despair; today a great international army of Socialists, marching irresistibly on and growing daily in number, organization, discipline, insight and assurance of victory. If even this mighty army of the proletariat has still not reached its goal, if, a long way from winning victory with one mighty stroke, it has slowly to press forward from position to position in a hard, tenacious struggle, this only proves, once and for all, how impossible it was in 1848 to win social reconstruction by a simple surprise attack.

A bourgeoisie split into two monarchist sections adhering to two dynasties,[5] a bourgeoisie, however, which demanded, above all, peace and security for its financial operations, faced with a proletariat vanquished, indeed, but still a constant menace, a proletariat round which petty bourgeois and peasants grouped themselves more and more—the continual threat of a violent outbreak, which, nevertheless, offered no prospect of a final solution—such was the situation, as if created for the *coup d'état* of the third, the pseudo-democratic pretender, Louis Bonaparte. On December 2, 1851, by means of the army, he put an end to the tense situation and secured for Europe the assurance of domestic tranquility, in order to give it the blessing of a new era of wars.[6] The period of revolutions from below was concluded for the time being; there followed a period of revolutions from above.

The imperial reaction of 1851 gave a new proof of the unripeness of the proletarian aspirations of that time. But it was itself to create the conditions under which they were bound to ripen. Internal tranquillity ensured the full development of the new industrial boom; the necessity of keeping the army occupied and of diverting the revolutionary currents outwards produced wars, in which Bonaparte, under the pretext of asserting "the principle of nationality," sought to sneak annexations for France. His imitator, Bismarck, adopted the same policy for Prussia; he made his *coup d'état*, his revolution from above, in 1886, against the German Confederation and Austria, and no less against the Prussian *Konfliktskammer*.* But Europe was too small for two Bonapartes and historical irony so willed it that Bismarck overthrew Bonaparte, and King William of Prussia not only established the little German Empire, but also the French Republic.[7] The general result, however, was that in Europe the autonomy and internal unity of the great nations, with the exception of Poland, had become a fact. Within relatively modest limits, it is true, but, for all that, on a scale large enough to allow the development of the working class to proceed without finding national complications any longer a serious obstacle. The grave-diggers of the Revolution of 1848 had become the executors of its will. And alongside of them rose threaten-

* *Konfliktskammer, i.e.,* the Prussian Chamber then in conflict with the government.

ingly the heir of 1848, the proletariat, in the International.

After the war of 1870-71, Bonaparte vanishes from the stage and Bismarck's mission is fulfilled, so that he can now sink back again into the ordinary *Junker*. The period, however, is brought to a close by the Paris Commune. An underhand attempt by Thiers to steal the cannon of the Paris National Guard, called forth a victorious rising. It was shown once more that, in Paris, none but a proletarian revolution is any longer possible. After the victory power fell, wholly of its own accord and quite undisputed, into the hands of the working class. And once again, twenty years after the time described in this work of ours, it was proved how impossible, even then, was this rule of the working class. On the one hand, France left Paris in the lurch, looked on while it bled from the bullets of MacMahon; on the other hand, the Commune was consumed in unfruitful strife between the two parties which divided it, the Blanquists (the majority) and the Proudhonists (the minority), neither of which knew what was to be done.

The victory which came as a gift in 1871 remained just as unfruitful as the surprise attack of 1848.

It was believed that the militant proletariat had been finally buried with the Paris Commune. But, completely to the contrary, it dates its most powerful advance from the Commune and the Franco-German war. The recruitment of the whole of the population able to bear arms into armies that could be counted in millions, and the introduction of firearms, projectiles and explosives of hitherto undreamt of efficacy created a complete revolution in all warfare. This, on the one hand, put a sudden end to the bonapartist war period and insured peaceful industrial development, since any war other than a world war of unheard of cruelty and absolutely incalculable outcome had become an impossibility. On the other hand, it caused military expenditure to rise in geometrical progression, and thereby forced up taxes to exorbitant levels and so drove the poorer classes of people into the arms of Socialism. The annexation of Alsace-Lorraine, the most immediate cause of the mad competition in armaments, might set the French and German bourgeoisie chauvinistically at

each other's throats; for the workers of the two countries it became a new bond of unity. And the anniversary of the Paris
Commune became the first universal commemoration day of the
whole proletariat.

The war of 1870-71 and the defeat of the Commune had
transferred the center of gravity of the European workers'
movement for the time being from France to Germany, as Marx
foretold. In France it naturally took years to recover from the
bloodletting of May, 1871.[8] In Germany, on the other hand,
where industry was, in addition, furthered (in positively hot-
house fashion) by the blessing of the French milliards and developed more and more quickly, Social-Democracy experienced
a much more rapid and enduring growth. Thanks to the understanding with which the German workers made use of the universal suffrage introduced in 1866, the astonishing growth of
the Party is made plain to all the world by incontestable figures.
1871, 102,000; 1874, 352,000; 1877, 493,000 Social-Democratic votes. Then came recognition of this advance by high
authority in the shape of the Anti-Socialist Law: the Party was
temporarily disrupted; the number of votes sank to 312,000 in
1881. But that was quickly overcome, and then, though op-
pressed by the Exceptional Law, without press, without external
organization and without the right of combination or meeting,
the rapid expansion really began: 1884, 550,000; 1887, 763,000;
1890, 1,427,000 votes. Then the hand of the state was paralyzed.
The Anti-Socialist Law disappeared; socialist votes rose to 1,-
787,000, over a quarter of all the votes cast. The government
and the ruling classes had exhausted all their expedients—
uselessly, to no purpose, and without success. The tangible
proofs of their impotence, which the authorities, from night
watchman to the imperial chancellor, had had to accept—and
that from the despised workers—these proofs were counted in
millions. The state was at the end of its Latin, the workers only
at the beginning of theirs.

But the German workers did a second great service to their
cause in addition to the first, which they rendered by their mere
existence as the strongest, best disciplined and most rapidly

growing Socialist Party. They supplied their comrades of all countries with a new weapon, and one of the sharpest, when they showed them how to use universal suffrage.

There had long been universal suffrage in France, but it had fallen into disrepute through the misuse to which the Bonapartist government had put it. After the Commune there was no workers' party to make use of it. Also in Spain it had existed since the republic, but in Spain boycott of the elections was ever the rule of all serious opposition parties. The Swiss experiences of universal suffrage, also, were anything but encouraging for a workers' party. The revolutionary workers of the Latin countries had been wont to regard the suffrage as a snare, as an instrument of government trickery. It was otherwise in Germany. *The Communist Manifesto* had already proclaimed the winning of universal suffrage, of democracy, as one of the first and most important tasks of the militant proletariat, and Lassalle had again taken up this point. When Bismarck found himself compelled to introduce the franchise [9] as the only means of interesting the mass of the people in his plans, our workers immediately took it in earnest and sent August Bebel to the first, constituent Reichstag. And from that day on, they have used the franchise in a way which has paid them a thousandfold and has served as a model to the workers of all countries. The franchise has been, in the words of the French Marxist program,[10] *"transformé, de moyen de deperie qu'il a été jusqu'ici, en instrument d'émancipation"*—they have transformed it from a means of deception, which it was heretofore, into an instrument of emancipation. And if universal suffrage had offered no other advantage than that it allowed us to count our numbers every three years; that by the regularly established, unexpectedly rapid rise in the number of votes it increased in equal measure the workers' certainty of victory and the dismay of their opponents, and so became our best means of propaganda; that it accurately informed us concerning our own strength and that of all hostile parties, and thereby provided us with a measure of proportion for our actions second to none, safeguarding us from untimely timidity as much as from untimely foolhardiness—if this had been the only

advantage we gained from the suffrage, then it would still have
been more than enough. But it has done much more than this.
In election agitation it provided us with a means, second to none,
of getting in touch with the mass of the people, where they still
stand aloof from us; of forcing all parties to defend their views
and actions against our attacks before all the people; and,
further, it opened to our representatives in the Reichstag a platform from which they could speak to their opponents in Parliament and to the masses without, with quite other authority and
freedom than in the press or at meetings. Of what avail to the
government and the bourgeoisie was their Anti-Socialist Law
when election agitation and socialist speeches in the Reichstag
continually broke through it?

With this successful utilization of universal suffrage, an entirely new mode of proletarian struggle came into force, and
this quickly developed further. It was found that the state institutions, in which the rule of the bourgeoisie is organized, offer
still further opportunities for the working class to fight these
very state institutions. They took part in elections to individual
diets, to municipal councils and to industrial courts; they con-
tested every post against the bourgeoisie in the occupation of
which a sufficient part of the proletariat had its say. And so
it happened that the bourgeoisie and the government came to be
much more afraid of the legal than of the illegal action of the
workers' party, of the results of elections than of those of rebellion.

For here, too, the conditions of the struggle had essentially
changed. Rebellion in the old style, the street fight with barricades, which up to 1848 gave everywhere the final decision, was
to a considerable extent obsolete.

Let us have no illusions about it: a real victory of an insurrection over the military in street fighting, a victory as between
two armies, is one of the rarest exceptions. But the insurgents,
also, counted on it just as rarely. For them it was solely a question of making the troops yield to moral influences, which, in
a fight between the armies of two warring countries do not
come into play at all, or do so to a much less degree. If they

succeed in this, then the troops fail to act, or the commanding officers lose their heads, and the insurrection wins. If they do not succeed in this, then, even where the military are in the minority, the superiority of better equipment and training, of unified leadership, of the planned employment of the military forces and of discipline makes itself felt. The most that the insurrection can achieve in actual tactical practice is the correct construction and defense of a single barricade. Mutual support; the disposition and employment of reserves; in short, the co-operation and harmonious working of the individual detachments, indispensable even for the defense of one quarter of the town, not to speak of the whole of a large town, are at best defective, and mostly not attainable at all; concentration of the military forces at a decisive point is, of course impossible. Hence the passive defense is the prevailing form of fight: the attack will rise here and there, but only by way of exception, to occasional advances and flank assaults; as a rule, however, it will be limited to occupation of the positions abandoned by the retreating troops. In addition, the military have, on their side, the disposal of artillery and fully equipped corps of skilled engineers, resources of war which, in nearly every case, the insurgents entirely lack. No wonder, then, that even the barricade struggles conducted with the greatest heroism—Paris, June 1848; Vienna, October 1848; Dresden, May 1849—ended with the defeat of the insurrection, so soon as the leaders of the attack, unhampered by political considerations, acted from the purely military standpoint, and their soldiers remained reliable.

The numerous successes of the insurgents up to 1848 were due to a great variety of causes. In Paris in July 1830 and February 1848, as in most of the Spanish street fights, there stood between the insurgents and the military a civic militia,[11] which either directly took the side of the insurrection, or else by its lukewarm, indecisive attitude caused the troops likewise to vacillate, and supplied the insurrection with arms into the bargain. Where this citizens' guard opposed the insurrection from the outset, as in June 1848 in Paris, the insurrection was vanquished. In Berlin in 1848, the people were victorious partly through a considerable accession of new fighting forces during the night and the morning of the 19th, partly as a result of the exhaustion and bad victualing of the troops, and, finally, partly as a result of the paralyzed command. But in all cases the fight was won because the troops failed to obey, because the officers had lost their power of decision or because their hands were tied.

Even in the classic time of street fighting, therefore, the barricade produced more of a moral than a material effect. It was a means of shaking the steadfastness of the military. If it held out until this was attained, then victory was won; if not, there was defeat. [*This is the main point, which must be kept in view, likewise when the chances of contingent future street fights are examined.*]

The chances, however, were in 1849 already pretty poor. Everywhere the bourgeoisie had thrown in its lot with the governments, "culture and property" had hailed and feasted the military moving against the insurrections. The spell of the barricade was broken; the soldier no longer saw behind it "the people," but rebels, agitators, plunderers, levelers, the scum of society; the officer had in the course of time become versed in the tactical forms of street fighting, he no longer marched straight ahead and without cover against the improvised breastwork, but went round it through gardens, yards and houses. And this was now successful, with a little skill, in nine cases out of ten.

But since then there have been very many more changes, and all in favor of the military. If the big towns have become considerably bigger, the armies have become bigger still. Paris and Berlin have, since 1848, grown less than fourfold, but their garrisons have grown more than that. By means of the railways, the garrisons can, in twenty-four hours, be more than doubled, and in forty-eight hours they can be increased to huge armies. The arming of this enormously increased number of troops has become incomparably more effective. In 1848 the smooth-bore percussion muzzle-loader, today the small-caliber magazine breech-loading rifle, which shoots four times as far, ten times as accurately and ten times as fast as the former. At that time the relatively ineffective round-shot and grape-shot of the artillery; today the percussion shells, of which one is sufficient to demolish the best barricade. At that time the pick-ax of the sapper for breaking through walls; today the dynamite cartridge.

On the other hand, all the conditions on the insurgents' side have grown worse. An insurrection with which all sections of the people sympathize, will hardly recur; in the class struggle all the middle sections will never group themselves round the proletariat so exclusively that the reactionary parties gathered round the bourgeoisie well-nigh disappear. The "people," therefore, will always appear divided, and with this a powerful lever, so extraordinarily effective in 1848, is lacking. Even if more soldiers who have seen service were to come over to the insurrectionists, the arming of them becomes so much the more difficult. The hunting and luxury guns of the gunshops—even if not previously made unusable by removal of part of the lock by the police—are far from being a match for the magazine rifle of the soldier, even in close fighting. Up to 1848 it was possible to make the necessary ammunition oneself out of powder and lead; today the cartridges differ for each rifle, and are everywhere alike only in one point, that they are a special product of big industry, and therefore not to be prepared *ex tempore*,* with the result that most rifles are useless as long as one does not possess the ammunition specially suited to them. And, finally, since 1848 the newly built quarters of the big towns have been laid out in long, straight, broad streets, as though made to give full effect to the new cannons and rifles. The revolutionary would have to be mad, who himself chose the working class districts in the North and East of Berlin for a barricade fight. [*Does that mean that in the future the street fight will play no further role? Certainly not. It only means that the conditions since 1848 have become far more unfavorable for civil fights, far more favorable for the military. A future street fight can therefore only be victorious when this unfavorable situation is compensated by other factors. Accordingly, it will occur more seldom in the beginning of a great revolution than in its further*

* On the spur of the moment.

progress, and will have to be undertaken with greater forces. These, however, may then well prefer, as in the whole Great French Revolution on September 4 and October 31, 1870,[12] *in Paris, the open attack to the passive barricade tactics.*]

Does the reader now understand, why the ruling classes decidedly want to bring us to where the guns shoot and the sabers slash? Why they accuse us today of cowardice, because we do not betake ourselves without more ado into the street, where we are certain of defeat in advance? Why they so earnestly implore us to play for once the part of cannon fodder?

The gentlemen pour out their prayers and their challenges for nothing, for nothing at all. We are not so stupid. They might just as well demand from their enemy in the next war that he should take up his position in the line formation of old Fritz,[13] or in the columns of whole divisions *à la* Wagram [14] and Waterloo, and with the flintlock in his hands at that. If the conditions have changed in the case of war between nations, this is no less true in the case of the class struggle. The time of surprise attacks, of revolutions carried through by small conscious minorities at the head of unconscious masses, is past. Where it is a question of a complete transformation of the social organization, the masses themselves must also be in it, must themselves already have grasped what is at stake, what they are going in for [*with body and soul*]. The history of the last fifty years has taught us that. But in order that the masses may understand what is to be done, long, persistent work is required, and it is just this work which we are now pursuing, and with a success which drives the enemy to despair.

In the Latin countries, also, it is being more and more recognized that the old tactics must be revised. Everywhere [*the unprepared onslaught has gone into the background, everywhere*] the German example of utilizing the suffrage, of winning all posts accessible to us, has been imitated. In France, where for more than a hundred years the ground has been undermined by revolution after revolution, where there is no single party which has not done its share in conspiracies, insurrections and all other revolutionary actions; in France, where, as a result, the government is by no means sure of the army and where, in general, the conditions for an insurrectionary *coup de main* * are far more favorable than in Germany—even in France the Socialists are realizing more and more that no lasting victory is possible for them, unless they first win the great mass of the people, *i.e.*, in this case, the peasants. Slow propaganda work and parliamentary activity are being recognized here, too, as the most immediate tasks of the Party. Successes were not lacking. Not only have a whole series of municipal councils been won; fifty Socialists have seats in the Chambers, and they have already overthrown three ministers and a President of the Republic. In Belgium last year the workers enforced the franchise, and have been victorious in a quarter of the constituencies. In Switzerland, in Italy, in Denmark, yes, even in Bulgaria and Rumania the Socialists are represented in the Parliaments. In Austria all parties agree that our admission to the Reichsrat † can no longer be withheld. We will get in, that is certain, the only question still in dispute is: by which door? And even in Russia, when the famous *Zemsky Sobor* meets, that National Assembly to which young Nicholas offers such vain resistance, even there we can reckon with certainty on also being represented in it.

Of course, our foreign comrades do not renounce their right to revolution. The right to revolution is, after all, the only real "historical right" the only right on which all modern states without exception rest, Mecklenburg included, whose aristocratic revolution was ended in 1755 by the "hereditary settlement," the glorious charter of feudalism still valid today. The right to revolution is so incontestably recognized in the general consciousness that even General von Boguslawski derives the right to a *coup d'état*, which he vindicates for his Kaiser, solely from this popular right.

But whatever may happen in other countries, German Social-Democracy has a special situation and therewith, at least in the first instance, a special task. The two million voters, whom it sends to the ballot box, together with the young men and

---

* Sudden attack.
† Parliament of the Austrian Empire.

women, who stand behind them as non-voters, form the most numerous, most compact mass, the decisive *"shock force"* of the international proletarian army. This mass already supplies over a fourth of the recorded votes; and as the by-elections to the Reichstag, the diet elections in individual states, the municipal council and industrial court elections demonstrate, it increases uninterruptedly. Its growth proceeds as spontaneously, as steadily, as irresistibly, and at the same time as tranquilly as a natural process. All government interventions have proved powerless against it. We can count even today on two and a half million voters. If it continues in this fashion, by the end of the century we shall conquer the greater part of the middle section of society, petty bourgeois and small peasants, and grow into the decisive power in the land, before which all other powers will have to bow, whether they like it or not. To keep this growth going without interruption until of itself it gets be· yond the control of the ruling governmental system [*not to fritter away this daily increasing shock force in advance guard fighting, but to keep it intact until the day of the decision,*] that is our main task. And there is only one means by which the steady rise of the socialist fighting forces in Germany could be momentarily halted, and even thrown back for some time: a clash on a big scale with the military, a bloodbath like that of 1871 in Paris. In the long run that would also be overcome. To shoot out of the world a party which numbers millions—all the magazine rifles of Europe and America are not enough for this. But the normal development would be impeded, [*the shock force would, perhaps, not be available at the critical moment,*] the decisive struggle * would be delayed, protracted and attended by heavy sacrifices.

The irony of world history turns everything upside down. We, the "revolutionaries," the "rebels"—we are thriving far better on legal methods than on illegal methods and revolt. The parties of order, as they call themselves, are perishing under the legal conditions created by themselves. They cry de-

---

* In the falsified text, the words *"die Entscheidung"* (the decision) have been substituted for *"der Entscheidungskampf"* (the decisive struggle).

spairingly with Odilon Barrot: *la légalité nous tue*, legality is the death of us; whereas we, under this legality, get firm muscles and rosy cheeks and look like eternal life. And if we are not so crazy as to let ourselves be driven into street fighting in order to please them, then nothing else is finally left for them but themselves to break through this legality so fatal to them.

Meanwhile they make new laws against revolution. Again everything is turned upside down. These anti-revolt fanatics of today, are they not themselves the rebels of yesterday? Have we, perchance, evoked the civil war of 1866? Have we driven the King of Hanover, the Elector of Hesse, the Duke of Nassau from their hereditary, lawful domains, and annexed these hereditary domains? And do these rebels against the German Confederation and three crowns by the grace of God complain of overthrow? *Quis tulerit Gracchos de seditione querentes?* * Who could allow the Bismarck worshipers to rail at revolt?

Let them, nevertheless, put through their anti-revolt bills, make them still worse, transform the whole penal law into india-rubber, they will achieve nothing but a new proof of their impotence. In order seriously to hit Social-Democracy, they will have to resort to quite other measures. They can only hold in check the Social-Democratic revolt which is just now doing so well by keeping within the law, by revolt on the part of the parties of order, which cannot live without breaking the laws. Herr Rössler, the Prussian bureaucrat, and Herr von Boguslawski, the Prussian general, have shown them the only way in which the workers, who refuse to let themselves be lured into street fighting, can still, perhaps, be held in check. Breach of the constitution, dictatorship, return to absolutism, *regis voluntas suprema lex!* † Therefore, only courage, gentlemen; here is no backing out of it; here you are in for it!

But do not forget that the German Empire, just as all small states and generally, all modern states, is a product of contract; of the contract, firstly, of the princes with one another and, secondly, of the princes with the people. If one side breaks the

* Who would suffer the Gracchi to complain of sedition?
† The King's will is the supreme law.

contract, the whole contract falls to the ground; the other side is then also no longer bound [*as Bismarck showed us so beautifully in 1866. If, therefore, you break the constitution of the Reich, then the Social-Democracy is free, can do and refrain from doing what it will as against you. But what it will do then it will hardly give away to you today!*].

It is now, almost to the year, sixteen hundred years since a dangerous party of revolt made a great commotion in the Roman Empire. It undermined religion and all the foundations of the state; it flatly denied that Cæsar's will was the supreme law; it was without a fatherland, international; it spread over all countries of the Empire from Gaul to Asia, and beyond the frontiers of the Empire. It had long carried on an underground agitation in secret; for a considerable time, however, it had felt itself strong enough to come out into the open. This party of revolt, which was known by the name of Christians, was also strongly represented in the army; whole legions were Christian. When they were ordered to attend the sacrificial ceremonies of the pagan established church, in order to do the honors there, the soldier rebels had the audacity to stick peculiar emblems— crosses—on their helmets in protest. Even the wonted barrack cruelties of their superior officers were fruitless. The Emperor Diocletian could no longer quietly look on while order, obedience and discipline in his army were being undermined. He intervened energetically, while there was still time. He passed an anti-Socialist, I should say anti-Christian, law. The meetings of the rebels were forbidden, their meeting halls were closed or even pulled down, the Christian badges, crosses, etc., were, like the red handkerchiefs in Saxony, prohibited. Christians were declared incapable of holding offices in the state, they were not to be allowed even to become corporals. Since there were not available at that time judges so well trained in "respect of persons" as Herr von Köller's anti-revolt bill[15] assumes, the Christians were forbidden out of hand to seek justice before a court. This exceptional law was also without effect. The Christians tore it down from the walls with scorn; they are even supposed to have burnt the Emperor's palace in Nicomedia over his head.

Then the latter revenged himself by the great persecution of Christians in the year 303, according to our chronology. It was the last of its kind. And it was so effective that seventeen years later the army consisted overwhelmingly of Christians, and the succeeding autocrat of the whole Roman Empire, Constantine, called the Great by the priests, proclaimed Christianity as the state religion.

London, March 6, 1895

The Class Struggles in France

I

FROM FEBRUARY TO JUNE 1848

(*From Number I*)

With the exception of a few short chapters, every important part of the annals of the revolution from 1848 to 1849 carries the heading: Defeat of the revolution!

But what succumbed in these defeats was not the revolution. It was the pre-revolutionary traditional appendages, results of social relationships, which had not yet come to the point of sharp class antagonisms—persons, illusions, conceptions, projects, from which the revolutionary party before the February Revolution was not free, from which it could be freed, not by the victory of February, but only by a series of defeats.

In a word: revolutionary advance made headway not by its immediate tragi-comic achievements, but on the contrary by the creation of a powerful, united counter-revolution, by the creation of an opponent, by fighting whom the party of revolt first ripened into a real revolutionary party.

To prove this is the task of the following pages.

THE DEFEAT OF JUNE 1848

After the July Revolution, when the Liberal banker, Laffitte, led his godfather, the Duke of Orleans, in triumph to the Hôtel de Ville,* he let fall the words: "From now on the bankers will rule." Laffitte had betrayed the secret of the revolution.[16]

It was not the French bourgeoisie that ruled under Louis Philippe, but a fraction of it, bankers, stock exchange kings, railway kings, owners of coal and ironworks and forests, a

* Town Hall.

section of landed proprietors that rallied round them—the so-called finance aristocracy. It sat on the throne, it dictated laws in the Chambers, it conferred political posts from cabinet port-folios to the tobacco bureau.

The real industrial bourgeoisie formed part of the official op-position, *i.e.*, it was represented only as a minority in the Cham-bers. Its opposition was expressed all the more decisively, the more unalloyed the autocracy of the finance aristocracy became, and the more it itself imagined that its domination over the working-class was ensured after the mutinies of 1832, 1834 and 1839,[17] which had been drowned in blood. *Grandin,* the Rouen manufacturer, the most fanatical instrument of bourgeois reac-tion, in the Constituent Assembly, as well as in the legislative National Assembly,[18] was the most violent opponent of Guizot in the Chamber of Deputies. *Leon Faucher,* later renowned for his impotent endeavors to push himself forward as the Guizot of the French counter-revolution, in the last days of Louis Philippe, waged a war of the pen for industry against specula-tion and its train bearer, the government. *Bastiat* agitated against the ruling system in the name of Bordeaux [19] and the whole of wine-producing France.

The petty bourgeoisie of all degrees, and the peasantry also, were completely excluded from political power. Finally, in the official opposition or entirely outside the *pays légal,*[20] there were the ideological representatives and spokesmen of the above classes, their savants, lawyers, doctors, etc., in a word: their so-called talents.

The July monarchy, owing to its financial need, was de-pendent from the beginning on the big bourgeoisie, and its dependence on the big bourgeoisie was the inexhaustible source of a growing financial need. It was impossible to subordinate state administration to the interests of national production, with-out balancing the budget, establishing a balance between state expenses and income. And how was this balance to be estab-lished, without limiting state expenditure, *i.e.*, without encroach-ing on interests which were so many supports of the ruling system, and without redistributing taxes, *i.e.*, without putting a considerable share of the burden of taxes on the shoulders of the big bourgeoisie itself?

Rather the fraction of the bourgeoisie that ruled and legislated through the Chambers had a direct interest in state indebtedness. The state deficit was even the main object of its speculation and played the chief role in its enrichment. At the end of each year a new deficit. After expiry of four or five years a new loan. And every new loan offered new opportunities to the finance aristocracy for defrauding the state which was kept artificially on the verge of bankruptcy—it had to contract with the bankers under the most unfavorable conditions. Each new loan gave a further opportunity for plundering the public that had invested its capital in state bonds, by stock exchange manipulations into the secrets of which the government and the majority in the Chambers were admitted. In general, the fluctuation of state credits and the possession of state secrets gave the bankers and their associates in the Chambers and on the throne the possibility of evoking sudden, extraordinary fluctuations in the quotations of state bonds, the result of which was always bound to be the ruin of a mass of smaller capitalists and the fabulously rapid enrichment of the big gamblers. If the state deficit was in the direct interest of the ruling fraction of the bourgeoisie, then it is clear why extraordinary state expenditure in the last years of Louis Philippe's government was far more than double the extraordinary state expenditure under Napoleon, indeed reached a yearly sum of nearly 400,000,000 francs, whereas the whole annual export of France seldom attained a volume amounting to 750,000,000 francs. The enormous sums which, in this way, flowed through the hands of the state, facilitated, moreover, swindling contracts for deliveries, bribery, defalcations and all kinds of roguery. The defrauding of the state, just as it occurred on a large scale in connection with loans, was repeated in detail, in the state works. The relationship between Chamber and government multiplied itself as the relationship between individual departments and individual *entrepreneurs*.

In the same way as the ruling class exploited state expenditure in general and state loans, they exploited the building of railways. The Chambers piled the main burdens on the state, and secured the golden fruits to the speculating finance aristocracy. One recalls the scandals in the Chamber of Deputies, when by chance it came out that all the members of the majority, including a number of ministers, had taken part as shareholders in the very railway construction which as legislators they caused to be carried out afterwards at the cost of the state.

On the other hand, the smallest financial reform was wrecked by the influence of the bankers. For example, the postal reform. Rothschild protested. Was it permissible for the state to curtail sources of income out of which interest was to be paid on its ever increasing debt?

The July monarchy was nothing other than a joint stock company for the exploitation of French national wealth, the dividends of which were divided amongst ministers, Chambers, 240,000 voters and their adherents. Louis Philippe was the director of this company—Robert Macaire [21] on the throne. Trade, industry, agriculture, shipping, the interests of the industrial bourgeoisie, were bound to be continually prejudiced and endangered under this system. The bourgeoisie in the July days had inscribed on its banner: *gouvernement à bon marché*, cheap government.

While the finance aristocracy made the laws, was at the head of the administration of the State, had command of all the organized public powers, dominated public opinion through facts and through the press, the same prostitution, the same shameless cheating, the same mania to get rich was repeated in every sphere, from the Court to the Café Borgne,[22] to get rich not by production, but by pocketing the already available wealth of others. In particular there broke out, at the top of bourgeois society, an unbridled display of unhealthy and dissolute appetites, which clashed every moment with the bourgeois laws themselves, wherein the wealth having its source in gambling naturally seeks its satisfaction, where pleasure becomes *crapuleux*,* where gold, dirt and blood flow together. The finance aristocracy, in its mode of acquisition as well as in its pleasures,

* Debauched.

is nothing but the resurrection of the lumpenproletariat at the top of bourgeois society.

And the non-ruling sections of the French bourgeoisie cried: corruption! The people cried: *à bas les grands voleurs! à bas les assassins!* * when in 1847, on the most prominent stages of bourgeois society, the same scenes were publicly enacted which regularly lead the lumpenproletariat to brothels, to workhouses and lunatic asylums, before the Bench, to bagnos and to the scaffold. The industrial bourgeoisie saw its interests endangered, the petty bourgeoisie was filled with moral indignation, the imagination of the people was offended, Paris was flooded with pamphlets—*"la dynastie Rothschild," "les juifs rois de l'epoque"* etc.†—in which the rule of the finance aristocracy was denounced and stigmatized with greater or less wit.

Rien pour la gloire! Glory brings no profit! *La paix partout et toujours!* ‡ War depresses the quotations of the Three and Four per Cents! the France of the Bourse Jews had inscribed on her banner. Her foreign policy was therefore lost in a series of mortifications to French national feeling, which reacted all the more vigorously when the robbery of Poland was brought to an end with the annexation of Cracow by Austria, and when Guizot came out actively on the side of the Holy Alliance [23] in the Swiss separatist war. The victory of the Swiss liberals in this mimic war raised the self-respect of the bourgeois opposition in France; the bloody uprising of the people in Palermo worked like an electric shock on the paralyzed masses of the people and awoke their great revolutionary memories and passions.¶

The eruption of the general discontent was finally accelerated and the sentiment for revolt ripened by two economic world-events.

* Down with the big thieves, down with the assassins!

† The Rothschild dynasty, the Jewish kings of the epoch.

‡ Peace everywhere and always.

¶ Annexation of Cracow by Austria in agreement with Russia and Prussia on November 11, 1846.—Swiss separatist war, November 4 to 22, 1847.—Rising in Palermo January 22, 1848; end of January nine days' bombardment of the town by the Neapolitans. [Note by Frederick Engels.]

The potato blight and the bad harvests of 1845 and 1846 increased the general ferment among the people. The high cost of living of 1847 called forth bloody conflicts in France as well as on the rest of the Continent. As against the shameless orgies of the finance aristocracy, the struggle of the people for the first necessities of life! At Buzançais the hunger rioters executed; [24] in Paris the over-satiated *escrocs* * snatched from the courts by the Royal family.

The second great economic event which hastened the outbreak of the revolution, was a general commercial and industrial crisis in England. Already heralded in the autumn of 1845 by the wholesale reverses of the speculators in railway shares, delayed during 1846 by a number of incidents such as the impending abolition of the corn duties, in the autumn of 1847 the crisis finally burst forth with the bankruptcy of the London grocers, on the heels of which followed the insolvencies of the land banks and the closing of the factories in the English industrial districts. The after-effect of this crisis on the Continent had not yet spent itself when the February Revolution broke out.

The devastation of trade and industry caused by the economic epidemic made the autocracy of the finance aristocracy still more unbearable. Throughout the whole of France the bourgeois opposition evoked the banquet agitation for an electoral reform which should win for them the majority of the Chambers and overthrow the Ministry of the Bourse. In Paris the industrial crisis had, in particular, the result of throwing a number of manufacturers and big traders, who under the existing circumstances could no longer do any business in the foreign market, onto the home market. They set up large establishments, the competition of which ruined the *épiciers* and *boutiquiers* † *en masse*. Hence the innumerable bankruptcies among this section of the Paris bourgeoisie, and hence their revolutionary action in February. It is known how Guizot and the Chambers answered the reform proposals with a plain challenge,[25] how Louis Philippe too late resolved on a Ministry led by Bar-

* Swindlers.
† Grocers and shopkeepers.

rot,[26] how hand-to-hand fighting took place between the people and the army, how the army was disarmed by the passive conduct of the National Guard, how the July monarchy had to give way to a Provisional Government.

The Provisional Government which emerged from the February barricades, necessarily mirrored in its composition the different parties which shared in the victory. It could not be anything but a compromise between the different classes which together had overturned the July throne, but whose interests were mutually antagonistic. A large majority of its members consisted of representatives of the bourgeoisie. The republican petty bourgeoisie were represented by Ledru-Rollin and Flocon, the republican bourgeoisie by the people from the *National*,[27] the dynastic opposition [28] by Cremieux, Dupont de l'Eure, etc. The working class had only two representatives, Louis Blanc and Albert. Finally, Lamartine as a member of the Provisional Government; that was actually no real interest, no definite class that was the February Revolution itself, the common uprising with its illusions, its poetry, its imagined content and its phrases. For the rest, the spokesman of the February Revolution, by his position and his views, belonged to the bourgeoisie.

If Paris, as a result of political centralization, rules France, the workers, in moments of revolutionary earthquakes, rule Paris. The first act in the life of the Provisional Government was an attempt to escape from this overpowering influence, by an appeal from intoxicated Paris to sober France. Lamartine disputed the right of the barricade fighters to proclaim the republic, on the ground that only the majority of Frenchmen had that right; they must await their votes, the Parisian proletariat must not besmirch its victory by a usurpation. The bourgeoisie allowed the proletariat only one usurpation—that of fighting.

Up to noon on February 25, the republic had not yet been proclaimed; on the other hand, the whole of the Ministries had already been divided among the bourgeois elements of the Provisional Government and among the generals, bankers and lawyers of the *National*. But the workers were this time determined not to put up with any swindling like that of July 1830.[29]

They were ready to take up the fight anew and to enforce the republic by force of arms. With this message, Raspail betook himself to the Hôtel de Ville. In the name of the Parisian proletariat he commanded the Provisional Government to proclaim the republic; if this order of the people were not fulfilled within two hours, he would return at the head of 200,000 men. The bodies of the fallen were scarcely cold, the barricades were not yet cleared away, the workers not yet disarmed, and the only force which could be opposed to them was the National Guard. Under these circumstances the prudent state doubts and juristic scruples of conscience of the Provisional Government suddenly vanished. The interval of two hours had not expired before all the walls of Paris were resplendent with the tremendous historical words:

République française! Liberté, Egalité, Fraternité! *

Even the memory of the limited aims and motives which drove the bourgeoisie into the February Revolution was extinguished by the proclamation of the republic on the basis of universal suffrage. Instead of a few small fractions of the bourgeoisie, whole classes of French society were suddenly hurled into the circle of political power, forced to leave the boxes, the stalls and the gallery and to act in person upon the revolutionary stage! With the constitutional monarchy the semblance of a state power independently confronting bourgeois society also vanished, as well as the whole series of subordinate struggles which this semblance of power called forth!

The proletariat, by dictating the republic to the Provisional Government and through the Provisional Government to the whole of France, stepped into the foreground forthwith as an independent party, but at the same time challenged the whole of bourgeois France to enter the lists against it. What it won was the terrain for the fight for its revolutionary emancipation, but in no way this emancipation itself!

The first thing that the February republic had to do was rather to complete the rule of the bourgeoise by allowing, be-

* French Republic! Liberty, Equality, Fraternity!

sides the finance aristocracy, all the propertied classes to enter the circle of political power. The majority of the great land-owners, the Legitimists, were emancipated from the political nullity to which they had been condemned by the July Mon-archy. Not for nothing had the *Gazette de France* [30] agitated in common with the opposition papers, not for nothing had Laroche-Jaquelin taken the side of the revolution in the session of the Chamber of Deputies on February 24th. The nominal proprietors, who form the great majority of the French people, the peasants, were put by universal suffrage in the position of arbiters of the fate of France. The February republic finally brought the rule of the bourgeoisie clearly into prominence, since it struck off the crown behind which Capital kept itself concealed.

Just as the workers in the July days had fought and won the bourgeois monarchy, so in the February days they fought and won the bourgeois republic. Just as the July monarchy had to proclaim itself as a monarchy surrounded by republican institu-tions, so the February republic was forced to proclaim itself a republic surrounded by social institutions. The Parisian prole-tariat compelled this concession, too.

Marche, a worker, dictated the decree by which the newly formed Provisional Government pledged itself to secure the existence of the workers by work, to provide work for all citi-zens, etc. And when, a few days later, it forgot its promises and seemed to have lost sight of the proletariat, a mass of 20,000 workers marched on the Hôtel de Ville with the cry: Organization of labor! Formation of a special Ministry of La-bor! The Provisional Government, with reluctance and after long debates, nominated a permanent, special commission, charged with finding means of improving the lot of the work-ing classes! This commission consisted of delegates from the corporations of Parisian artisans and was presided over by Louis Blanc [31] and Albert. The Luxembourg was assigned to it as a meeting place. In this way the representatives of the working class were exiled from the seat of the Provisional Government, the bourgeois section of which held the real state power and the reins of administration exclusively in its hands, and side by side with the Ministries of Finance, Trade and Public Works, side by side with the banks and the bourse, there arose a socialist synagogue whose high priests, Louis Blanc and Albert, had the task of discovering the promised land, of preaching the new gospel and of occupying the attention of the Parisian proletariat. Unlike any profane state power, they had no budget, no executive authority at their disposal. With their heads they had to break the pillars of bourgeois society. While Luxembourg sought the philosopher's stone, in the Hôtel de Ville they minted the current coinage.

And yet the claims of the Parisian proletariat, so far as they went beyond the bourgeois republic, could win no other existence than the nebulous one of the Luxembourg.

In common with the bourgeoisie the workers had made the February Revolution, and alongside the bourgeoisie they sought to put through their interests, just as they had installed a worker in the Provisional Government itself alongside the bourgeois majority. Organization of labor! But wage labor is the existing, bourgeois organization of labor. Without it there is no capital, no bourgeoisie, no bourgeois society. Their own Ministry of Labor! But the Ministries of Finance, of Trade, of Public Works—are not these the bourgeois Ministries of Labor? And alongside these a proletarian Ministry of Labor must be a Ministry of impotence, a Ministry of pious wishes, a commission of the Luxembourg. Just as the workers thought to emancipate themselves side by side with the bourgeoisie, so they opined they would be able to consummate a proletarian revolution within the national walls of France, side by side with the remaining bourgeois nations. But French production relations are conditioned by the foreign trade of France, by her position on the world market and the laws thereof; how should France break them without a European revolutionary war, which would strike back at the despot of the world market, England?

A class in which the revolutionary interests of society are concentrated, so soon as it has risen up, finds directly in its own situation the content and the material of its revolutionary

activity: foes to be laid low, measures, dictated by the needs
of the struggle, to be taken; the consequences of its own deeds
drive it on. It makes no theoretical inquiries into its own task.
The French working class had not attained this standpoint; it
was still incapable of accomplishing its own revolution.

The development of the industrial proletariat is, in general,
conditioned by the development of the industrial bourgeoisie.
Only under its rule the proletariat wins the extensive national
existence, which can raise its revolution to a national one and
itself creates the modern means of production, which become
just so many means of its revolutionary emancipation. Only
bourgeois rule tears up the roots of feudal society and levels the
ground on which a proletarian revolution is alone possible. In
France industry is more developed and the bourgeoisie more
revolutionary than elsewhere on the Continent. But was not
the February Revolution directed immediately against the
finance aristocracy? This fact proved that the industrial bourgeoisie did not rule France. The industrial bourgeoisie can only
rule where modern industry shapes all property relations in conformity with itself, and industry can only win this power when
it has conquered the world market, for national bounds are not
wide enough for its development. But French industry, to a
great extent, maintains its command even of the national market
only through a more or less modified system of prohibitive
duties.[32] If, therefore, the French proletariat, at the moment of
a revolution, possesses in Paris actual power and influence which
spur it on to a drive beyond its means, in the rest of France it
is crowded into single, scattered industrial centers, being almost
lost in the superior numbers of peasants and petty bourgeois.
The struggle against capital in its developed, modern form, in
its culminating phase the struggle of the industrial wage worker
against the industrial bourgeois, is in France partially a fact,
which after the February days could supply the national content
of the revolution so much the less, since the struggle against
capital's secondary modes of exploitation, that of the peasants
against the usury in mortgages, of the petty bourgeois against
the wholesale dealer, banker and manufacturer, in a word,

against bankruptcy, was still hidden in the general uprising against the general finance aristocracy. Nothing is more understandable, then, than that the Paris proletariat sought to put through its own interests along with those of the bourgeoisie, instead of enforcing them as the revolutionary interests of society itself, and that it let the red flag be lowered to the tricolor.[38] The French workers could not take a step forward, could not touch a hair of the bourgeois order before the course of the revolution had forced the mass of the nation, peasants and petty bourgeois, standing between the proletariat and the bourgeoisie and in revolt not against this order, against the rule of capital, to attach itself to the proletariat as its vanguard. The workers could only buy this victory through the huge defeat of June.

To the Luxembourg commission, this creation of the Paris workers, remains the merit of having disclosed from the European tribune the secret of the revolution of the nineteenth century: the emancipation of the proletariat. The *Moniteur* raged when it had to propagate officially the "wild ravings" which up to that time lay buried in the apocryphal writings of the Socialists and only reached the ears of the bourgeoisie from time to time as remote, half terrifying, half ludicrous legends. Europe awoke astonished from its bourgeois doze. In the ideas of the proletarians, therefore, who confused the finance aristocracy with the bourgeoisie in general; in the imagination of good old republicans who denied the very existence of classes or, at most, admitted them as a result of the constitutional monarchy; in the hypocritical phrases of the sections of the bourgeoisie up till now excluded from power, the rule of the bourgeoisie was abolished with the introduction of the republic. All the royalists were transformed into republicans and all the millionaires of Paris into workers. The phrase which corresponded to this imagined liquidation of class relations was *fraternité*, universal fraternization and brotherhood. This pleasant abstraction from class antagonisms, this sentimental equalization of contradictory class interests, this fantastic elevation above the class struggle, *fraternité*, this was the special catch-cry of the February Revolution. The classes were divided by a mere misunderstanding and Lamartine baptized the Provisional Government on February 24 as *"un gouvernement qui suspende ce malentendu terrible qui existe entre les différentes classes."* * The Parisian proletariat reveled in this generous intoxication of fraternity.

The Provisional Government, on its side, once it was compelled to proclaim the republic, did everything to make it acceptable to the bourgeoisie and to the provinces. The bloody terror of the first French republic was disavowed by the abolition of the death penalty for political offenses; the press was opened to all opinions; the army, the courts, the administration remained with a few exceptions in the hands of their old dignitaries; none of the July monarchy's great offenders was brought to book. The bourgeois republicans of the *National* amused themselves by exchanging monarchist names and costumes for old republican ones. For them the republic was only a new ball dress for the old bourgeois society. The young republic sought its chief merit, not in being alarming, but rather in constantly taking fright itself, and through the soft compliance and non-resistance of its existence, sought to win existence and to disarm resistance. At home to the privileged classes, abroad to the despotic powers, it was loudly announced that the republic was of a peaceful nature. Live and let live was its motto. In addition thereto, shortly after the February Revolution the Germans, Poles, Austrians, Hungarians and Italians revolted,[34] each people in accordance with its immediate situation. Russia and England—the latter itself agitated,[35] the former cowed— were not prepared. The republic, therefore, had no national enemy. Consequently, there were no great foreign complications which could fire the energies, hasten the revolutionary process, drive the Provisional Government forward or throw it overboard. The Parisian proletariat, which recognized its own creation in the republic, naturally acclaimed each act of the Provisional Government which allowed it to take its place more

* A government that removes this terrible misunderstanding which exists between different classes.

easily in bourgeois society. It willingly allowed itself to be employed on police service by Caussidière, in order to protect property in Paris, just as it allowed Louis Blanc to arbitrate wage disputes between workers and masters. It was its *point d'honneur* * to preserve unblemished the bourgeois honor of the republic in the eyes of Europe.

The republic encountered no resistance either abroad or at home. It was thereby disarmed. Its task was no longer the revolutionary transformation of the world, it was only to adapt itself to the relations of bourgeois society. Concerning the fanaticism with which the Provisional Government undertook this task, there is no more eloquent testimony than its financial measures.

Public and private credit were naturally shattered. Public credit rests on confidence that the state will allow itself to be exploited by the Jews of finance. But the old state had vanished and the revolution was directed above all against the finance aristocracy. The vibrations of the last European commercial crisis had not yet ceased. Bankruptcy still followed bankruptcy.

Private credit was therefore paralyzed, circulation restricted, production at a standstill before the February Revolution broke out. The revolutionary crisis increased the commercial crisis. And if private credit rests on confidence that bourgeoise production to the full extent of its relations, that the bourgeois order, is untouched and inviolate, what effect must a revolution have had, which questioned the basis of bourgeois production, the economic slavery of the proletariat, and set up against the Bourse the sphinx of the Luxembourg? The uprising of the proletariat is the abolition of bourgeois credit; for it is the abolition of bourgeois production and its order. Public and private credit are the economic thermometer, by which the intensity of a revolution can be measured. To the same degree as they fall, the glow and generative force of the revolution rises.

The Provisional Government wanted to strip the republic of its anti-bourgeois appearance. And so it had, above all, to try to ensure the exchange value of this new form of state, its

* Point of honor.

quotation on the Bourse. With the current quotation of the republic on the Bourse, private credit necessarily rose again.

In order to turn aside the very suspicion that it would not or could not comply with the obligations assumed by the monarchy, in order to build up confidence in bourgeois morality and capacity to pay, the Provisional Government took refuge in a boast as undignified as it was childish. In advance of the legal date of payment they paid out 5 per cent, 4½ per cent and 4 per cent interest to the state creditors. The bourgeois aplomb, the self-respect of the capitalists suddenly awoke when they saw the anxious haste with which it was sought to buy their confidence.

The financial embarrassment of the Provisional Government was naturally not lessened by a theatrical stroke which robbed it of its stock of ready cash. The financial pinch could no longer be concealed and petty bourgeois, domestic servants and workers had to pay for the pleasant surprise which had been prepared for the state creditors.

The savings bank books with an amount of more than one hundred francs were declared no longer changeable into gold. The sums deposited in the savings banks were confiscated and by decree transformed into unredeemable state debt. This embittered the already hard pressed petty bourgeois against the republic. Since he received, in place of his savings bank books, state debt certificates, he was forced to go to the Bourse in order to sell them and in this way delivered himself directly into the hands of the Bourse Jews, against whom he had made the February Revolution.

The finance aristocracy which ruled under the July monarchy had its high church in the Bank. Just as the Bourse governs state credit, the Bank governs commercial credit.

The Bank, directly threatened not only in its rule, but in its very existence, by the February Revolution, tried from the beginning to discredit the republic by making the lack of credit general. It suddenly withdrew the credits of the bankers, the manufacturers and the merchants. This maneuver, as it did not immediately call forth a counter-revolution, necessarily reacted on the Bank itself. The capitalists drew out the money which they had deposited in the vaults of the Bank. The possessors of bank notes rushed the pay office in order to change them for gold and silver.

The Provisional Government could, without forcible interference, force the Bank into bankruptcy in a legal manner; it had only to remain passive and leave the Bank to its fate. The bankruptcy of the Bank—that was the deluge which in a trice would sweep away from French soil the finance aristocracy, the most powerful and dangerous enemy of the republic, the golden pedestal of the July monarchy. And once the Bank was bankrupt, the bourgeoisie itself would have to regard it as a last, desperate attempt at rescue if the government formed a national bank and subjected national credit to the control of the nation.

The Provisional Government, on the contrary, fixed a compulsory quotation for the notes of the Bank. It did more. It transformed all provincial banks into branches of the *Banque de France* * and allowed it to cast its net over the whole of France. Later it pledged the state forests to the Bank as a guarantee for a loan that it contracted from it. In this way the February Revolution directly strengthened and enlarged the bankocracy which it was to have overthrown.

Meanwhile the Provisional Government was bowed beneath the burden of a growing deficit. In vain it begged for patriotic sacrifices. Only the workers threw in their alms. Recourse had to be had to an heroic measure, to imposition of a new tax. But whom to tax? The Bourse wolves, the bank kings, the state creditors, the *rentiers*, the manufacturers? That was not the way to ingratiate the republic with the bourgeoisie. That meant, on the one hand, to endanger state credit and commercial credit, which, on the other hand, it was sought to purchase with such great sacrifices and humiliations. But someone had to fork out the cash. Who was sacrificed to bourgeois credit? *Jacques le bonhomme*,[36] the peasant.

The Provisional Government imposed an additional tax of 45

* Bank of France.

centimes in the franc on the four direct taxes. The government press humbugged the Paris proletariat into thinking that this tax would fall for preference on the big landed property, on the possessors of the milliard granted by the Restoration. But in truth it hit the peasant class above all, *i.e.*, the large majority of the French people. They had to pay the costs of the February Revolution; in them the counter-revolution gained its main material. The 45 centimes tax was a life question for the French peasant; he made it a life question for the republic. From that moment the republic meant the 45 centimes tax for the French peasant, and he saw in the Paris proletariat the spendthrift who did himself well at his expense.

Whereas the Revolution of 1789 began by shaking the feudal burdens off the peasants, the revolution of 1848 announced itself with a new tax on the rural population, in order not to endanger capital and keep its state machine going.[37]

There was only one means by which the Provisional Government could set aside all these inconveniences and jerk the state out of its old rut—the declaration of state bankruptcy. We recall how Ledru-Rollin in the National Assembly subsequently recited the virtuous indignation with which he repudiated this demand of the Bourse Jew, Fould, now French Finance Minister. Fould had handed him the apple from the tree of knowledge.

The Provisional Government, having honored the bill drawn on the state by the old bourgeois society, succumbed to the latter. It had become the hard-pressed debtor of bourgeois society instead of confronting it as the pressing creditor that had to collect the revolutionary debts of many years. It had to consolidate the shaky bourgeois relationship, in order to fulfill obligations which are only to be fulfilled within these relationships. Credit becomes a condition of life for it and the concessions to the proletariat, the promises made to it, become so many fetters which had to be struck off. The emancipation of the workers—even as a phrase—became an unbearable danger to the new republic, for it was a standing protest against the restoration of credit, which rests on undisturbed and untroubled recognition of the existing economic class relations. Therefore, it was necessary to have done with the workers.

The February Revolution had cast the army out of Paris. The National Guard, *i.e.*, the bourgeoisie in its different grades, formed the sole power. Alone, however, it did not feel itself a match for the proletariat. Moreover, it was forced slowly and bit by bit to open its ranks and allow armed proletarians to enter the National Guard, albeit after the most tenacious resistance and after setting up a hundred different obstacles. There consequently remained but one way out: to set one part of the proletariat against the other.

For this purpose the Provisional Government formed 24 battalions of Mobile Guards, each of a thousand men, out of young men from 15 to 20 years. They belonged for the most part to the *lumpenproletariat*, which, in all big towns form a mass strictly differentiated from the industrial proletariat, a recruiting ground for thieves and criminals of all kinds, living on the crumbs of society, people without a definite trade, vagabonds, *gens sans feu et sans aveu*,* with differences according to the degree of civilization of the nation to which they belong, but never renouncing their *lazzaroni* † character; at the youthful age at which the Provisional Government recruited them, thoroughly malleable, capable of the most heroic deeds and the most exalted sacrifices, as of the basest banditry and the dirtiest corruption. The Provisional Government paid them 1 franc 50 centimes a day, *i.e.*, it bought them. It gave them their own uniform, *i.e.*, it made them outwardly distinct from the blouse of the workers. They had assigned to them as leaders, partly officers from the standing army; partly they themselves elected young sons of the bourgeoisie whose rhodomontades about death for the fatherland and devotion to the republic captivated them.

And so the Paris proletariat was confronted with an army, drawn from its own midst, of 24,000 young, strong and foolhardy men. It gave cheers for the Mobile Guard on its marches through Paris. It recognized in it its champions of the barri-

---

* Folk without fire and without faith, *i.e.*, rabble.
† Lazzaroni: hoboes of Naples.

cades. It regarded it as the proletarian guard in opposition to the bourgeois National Guard. Its error was pardonable.

Besides the Mobile Guard, the Government decided to gather round itself an industrial army of workers. A hundred thousand workers thrown on the streets through the crisis and the revolution were enrolled by the Minister Marie in so-called National *Ateliers*.* Under this grand name was hidden nothing but the employment of the workers on tedious, monotonous, unproductive earthworks at a wage of 23 sous. English *workhouses* in the open—that is what these National *Ateliers* were. The Provisional Government believed that it had formed in them a second proletarian army against the workers themselves. This time the bourgeoisie was mistaken in the National *Ateliers*, just as the workers were mistaken in the Mobile Guard. It had created an army for mutiny.

But one purpose was achieved.

National *Ateliers*—that was the name of the people's workshops, which Louis Blanc preached in the Luxembourg. The *Ateliers* of Marie, devised in direct antagonism to the Luxembourg, thanks to the common name, offered occasion for a plot of errors worthy of the Spanish comedy of servants. The Provisional Government itself secretly spread the report that these National *Ateliers* were the discovery of Louis Blanc, and this seemed the more plausible because Louis Blanc, the prophet of the National *Ateliers*, was a member of the Provisional Government. And in the half naïve, half intentional confusion of the Paris bourgeoisie, in the artificially maintained opinion of France and of Europe, these workhouses were the first realization of socialism, which was put in the pillory with them.

In their title, though not in their content, the National *Ateliers* were the embodied protest of the proletariat against bourgeois industry, bourgeois credit and the bourgeois republic. The whole hate of the bourgeoisie was therefore turned upon them. At the same time, it had found in them the point against which it could direct the attack, as soon as it was strong enough to break openly with the February illusions. All the discontent,

* National Workshops.

all the ill humor of the petty bourgeois was simultaneously directed agianst these National *Ateliers*, the common target. With real fury they reckoned up the sums that the proletarian loafers swallowed, while their own situation became daily more unbearable. A state pension for sham labor, that is socialism! they growled to themselves. They sought the basis of their misery in the National *Ateliers*, the declarations of the Luxembourg, the marches of the workers through Paris. And no one was more fantastic about the alleged machinations of the Communists than the petty bourgeoisie who hovered hopelessly on the brink of bankruptcy.

Thus in the approaching *mêlée* between bourgeoisie and proletariat, all the advantages, all the decisive posts, all the middle sections of society were in the hands of the bourgeoisie, at the same time as the waves of the February Revolution rose high over the whole Continent, and each new post brought a new bulletin of revolution, now from Italy, now from Germany, now from the remotest parts of South-Eastern Europe, and maintained the general exuberance of the people, giving it constant testimony of a victory that it had already lost.

March 17 and April 16 were the days on which occurred the first skirmishes in the big class struggle which the bourgeois republic hid under its wings.

March 17 revealed the ambiguous situation of the proletariat, which permitted no decisive act. Its demonstration originally had the purpose of pushing the Provisional Government back onto the path of the revolution, of effecting the exclusion of its bourgeois members according to circumstances, and of compelling the postponement of the election days for the National Assembly and the National Guard. But on March 16 the bourgeoisie represented in the National Guard made a hostile demonstration against the Provisional Government. With the cry: *à bas Ledru-Rollin!* * it surged to the Hôtel de Ville. And the people was forced, on March 17, to shout: Long live Ledru-Rollin! Long live the Provisional Government! It was forced to take sides against the bourgeoisie with the party of the bour-

* Down with Ledru-Rollin.

geois republic, which seemed to it to be in danger. It strengthened the Provisional Government, instead of subordinating it to
itself. March 17 went off in a melodramatic scene, and if the
Paris proletariat on this day once more displayed its giant body,
the bourgeoisie both inside and outside the Provisional Government were all the more determined to break it.

April 16 was a misunderstanding organized by the Provisional
Government and the bourgeoisie. The workers had gathered
in great numbers in the Field of Mars and in the Hippodrome,
in order to prepare their selections for the general staff of
the National Guard. Suddenly throughout Paris, from one
end to the other, a rumor spread as quick as lightning, to the
effect that the workers had met, armed, in the Field of Mars,
under the leadership of Louis Blanc, Blanqui, Cabet and Raspail, in order to march thence on the Hôtel de Ville, overthrow
the Provisional Government and proclaim a Communist government. The general alarm is sounded—Ledru-Rollin, Marrast
and Lamartine later contended for the honor of having initiated
this—in an hour 100,000 men are under arms; the Hôtel de
Ville is occupied at all points by the National Guard; the cry:
Down with the Communists! Down with Louis Blanc, with
Blanqui, with Raspail, with Cabet! thunders throughout Paris,
and innumerable deputations pay homage to the Provisional
Government, all ready to save the fatherland and society. When
the workers finally appeared before the Hôtel de Ville, in
order to hand over to the Provisional Government a patriotic
collection which they had made in the Field of Mars, they
learn to their amazement that bourgeois Paris had defeated
their shadow in a very carefully calculated sham fight. The
terrible attempt of April 16 furnished the excuse for recalling
the army to Paris—the actual purpose of the clumsily constructed comedy—and for the reactionary federalist demonstrations in the provinces.

On May 4 the National Assembly met, the result of the direct
general elections. Universal suffrage did not possess the magic
power which republicans of the old school had ascribed to it.
They saw in the whole of France, at least in the majority of

Frenchmen, *citoyens* * with the same interests, the same understanding, etc. This was their cult of the people. Instead of
their imaginary people, the elections brought the real people
to the light of day, *i.e.*, representatives of the different classes
into which it falls. We have seen why peasants and petty bourgeois had to vote under the leadership of a bourgeoisie spoiling
for fight and big landowners frantic for restoration. But if
universal suffrage was not the miraculous magic wand for which
the republican duffers had taken it, it possessed the incomparably higher merit of unchaining the class struggle, of letting
the various middle sections of petty-bourgeois society rapidly
live through their illusions and disappointments, of tossing all
the fractions of the exploiting class at one throw to the head of
the state, and thus tearing from them their treacherous mask,
whereas the monarchy with its property qualification only let
definite fractions of the bourgeoisie compromise themselves, and
let the others lie hidden behind the scenes and surrounded them
with the halo of a common opposition.

In the Constituent National Assembly, which met on May
4, the Bourgeois republicans, the republicans of the *National*
had the upper hand. Legitimists and even Orleanists at first
only dared to show themselves under the mask of bourgeois
republicanism. Only in the name of the republic could the fight
against the proletariat be undertaken.

The republic dates from May 4, not from February 25, *i.e.*,
the republic recognized by the French people; it is not the republic which the Paris proletariat thrust upon the Provisional
Government, not the republic with social institutions, not the
dream picture which hovered before the fighters on the barricades. The republic proclaimed by the National Assembly, the
sole legitimate republic, is the republic which is no revolutionary weapon against the bourgeois order, but rather its political
reconstitution, the political reconsolidation of bourgeois society,
in a word, the bourgeois republic. From the tribune of the
National Assembly this contention resounded and in the entire
republican and anti-republican bourgeois press it found its echo.

* Citizens.

And we have seen how the February republic in reality was not and could not be other than a bourgeois republic; how the Provisional Government, nevertheless, was forced by the immediate pressure of the proletariat to announce it as a republic with social institutions, how the Paris proletariat was still incapable of going beyond the bourgeois republic otherwise than in ideas, in imagination; how it everywhere acted in its service when it really came to action; how the promises made to it became an unbearable danger for the new republic; how the whole life process of the Provisional Government was comprised in a continuous fight against the demands of the proletariat.

In the National Assembly all France sat in judgment on the Paris proletariat. It broke immediately with the social illusions of the February Revolution; it roundly proclaimed the bourgeois republic, nothing but the bourgeois republic. It at once excluded the representatives of the proletariat, Louis Blanc and Albert, from the Executive Commission appointed by it; it threw out the proposal of a special Labor Ministry, and received with stormy applause the statement of the Minister Trélat: "The question is merely one of bringing labor back to its old conditions."

But all this was not enough. The February republic was won by the workers with the passive support of the bourgeoisie. The proletarians regarded themselves, and rightly, as the victors of February, and they made the proud claims of victors. They had to be vanquished on the streets, they had to be shown that they were worsted as soon as they fought, not with the bourgeoisie, but against the bourgeoisie. Just as the February republic, with its socialist concessions, required a battle of the proletariat, united with the bourgeoisie, against monarchy, so a second battle was necessary in order to sever the republic from the socialist concessions, in order to officially work out the bourgeois republic as dominant. The bourgeoisie had to refute the demands of the proletariat with arms in its hands. And the real birthplace of the bourgeois republic is not the February victory; it is the June defeat.

The proletariat hastened the decision when, on the 15th of May, it pushed into the National Assembly, sought in vain to recapture its revolutionary influence and only delivered its energetic leaders to the jailers of the bourgeoisie.[38] *Il faut en finir!* This situation must end! With this cry the National assembly gave vent to its determination to force the proletariat into a decisive struggle. The Executive Commission issued a series of provocative decrees, such as that prohibiting congregation of the people, etc. From the tribune of the Constituent National Assembly, the workers were directly provoked, insulted and derided. But the real point of the attack was, as we have seen, the National *Ateliers*. The Constituent National Assembly imperiously pointed these out to the Executive Commission, which only waited to hear its own plan put forward as the command of the National Assembly.

The Executive Commission began by making entry into the National *Ateliers* more difficult, by turning the day wage into a piece wage, by banishing workers not born in Paris to Sologne, ostensibly for the construction of earthworks. These earthworks were only a rhetorical formula with which to gloss over their expulsion, as the workers, returning disillusioned, announced to their comrades. Finally, on June 21, a decree appeared in the *Moniteur*, which ordered the forcible expulsion of all unmarried workers from the National *Ateliers*, or their enrollment in the army.

The workers were left no choice: they had to starve or start to fight. They answered on June 22 with the tremendous insurrection in which the first great battle was joined between the two classes that split modern society. It was a fight for the preservation or annihilation of the bourgeois order. The veil that shrouded the republic was torn to pieces.

It is well known how the workers, with unexampled bravery and talent, without chiefs, without a common plan, without means and, for the most part, lacking weapons, held in check for five days the army, the Mobile Guard, the Parisian National Guard, and the National Guard that streamed in from the provinces. It is well known how the bourgeoisie compensated itself for the mortal anguish it underwent by unheard of brutality, and massacred over 3,000 prisoners.

The official representatives of French democracy were steeped in republican ideology to such an extent that it was only some weeks later that they began to have an inkling of the meaning of the June fight. They were stupefied by the gunpowder smoke in which their fantastic republic dissolved.

The immediate impression which the news of the June defeat made on us, the reader will allow us to describe in the words of the *N. Rh. Z.*: *

The last official remnant of the February Revolution, the Executive Commission, has melted away, like an apparition, before the seriousness of events. The fireworks of Lamartine have turned into the war rockets of Cavaignac. *Fraternité*, the fraternity of antagonistic classes of which one exploits the other, this *fraternité*, proclaimed in February, written in capital letters on the brow of Paris, on every prison, on every barracks— its true, unadulterated, its prosaic expression is civil war, civil war in its most fearful form, the war of labor and capital. This fraternity flamed in front of all the windows of Paris on the evening of June 25, when the Paris of the bourgeoisie was illuminated, whilst the Paris of the proletariat burnt, bled, moaned. Fraternity endured just as long as the interests of the bourgeoisie were in fraternity with the interests of the proletariat.— Pedants of the old revolutionary traditions of 1793; socialist doctrinaires who begged at the doors of the bourgeoisie on behalf of the people and were allowed to preach long sermons and to compromise themselves as long as the proletarian lion had to be lulled to sleep; republicans who demanded the old bourgeois order in its entirety, with the exception of the crowned head; adherents of the dynasty among the opposition upon whom fortune foisted the overthrow of the dynasty instead of a change of Ministers; Legitimists who wanted, not to throw away the livery, but to change its cut, these were the allies with whom the people made its February.— The February Revolution was the beautiful revolution, the revolution of universal sympathy, because the antagonisms, which had flared up in it against the monarchy, slumbered peacefully side by side, still undeveloped, because the social struggle which formed its background had won only a joyous existence, an existence of phrases, of words. The June revolution is the ugly revolution, the repulsive revolution, because things have taken

* *Neue Rheinische Zeitung.*

the place of phrases, because the republic uncovered the head of the
monster itself, by striking off the crown that shielded and concealed it.—
Order! was the battle cry of Guizot. Order! cried Sebastiani,[39] the fol-
lower of Guizot, when Warsaw became Russian. Order! shouts Cavaignac,
the brutal echo of the French National Assembly and of the republican
bourgeoisie. Order! thundered his grape-shot, as it ripped up the body of
the proletariat. None of the numerous revolutions of the French bourgeoisie since 1789 was an attack on order; for they allowed the rule of
the class, they allowed the slavery of the workers, they allowed the bourgeois order to endure, however often the political form of this rule and of
this slavery changed. June has attacked this order. Woe to June! (*N. Rh.
Z.*, June 29, 1848.)

Woe to June! re-echoes Europe.

The Paris proletariat was forced into the June insurrection
by the bourgeoisie. In this lay its doom. Neither its immediate,
admitted needs drove it to want to win the forcible overthrow
of the bourgeoisie, nor was it equal to this task. The *Moniteur*
had to inform it officially that the time was past when the
republic saw any occasion to do honor to its illusions, and its
defeat first convinced it of the truth that the slightest improve-
ment in its position remains an utopia within the bourgeois
republic, an utopia that becomes a crime as soon as it wants to
realize it. In place of its demands, exuberant in form, but petty
and even still bourgeois in content, the concession of which it
wanted to wring from the February republic, there appeared the
bold slogan of revolutionary struggle: Overthrow of the bourgeoisie! Dictatorship of the working class!

By making its burial place the birthplace of the bourgeois
republic the proletariat compelled the latter to come out forthwith in its pure form as the state whose admitted object is to
perpetuate the rule of capital, the slavery of labor. With constant regard to the scarred, irreconcilable, unconquerable enemy
—unconquerable because its existence is the condition of its own
life—bourgeois rule, freed from all fetters, was bound to turn
immediately into bourgeois terrorism. With the proletariat removed for the time being from the stage and bourgeois dictatorship recognized officially, the middle sections, in the mass,

had more and more to side with the proletariat as their position became more unbearable and their antagonism to the bourgeoisie became more acute. Just as earlier in its upsurge, so now they had to find in its defeat the cause of their misery.

If the June insurrection raised the self-reliance of the bourgeoisie all over the Continent, and caused it to league itself openly with the feudal monarchy against the people, what was the first sacrifice to this alliance? The Continental bourgeoisie itself. The June defeat prevented it from consolidating its rule and from bringing the people, half satisfied and half out of humor, to a standstill at the lowest stage of the bourgeois revolution.

Finally, the defeat of June divulged to the despotic powers of Europe the secret that France under all conditions must maintain peace abroad in order to be able to wage civil war at home. Thus the peoples who had begun the fight for their national independence were abandoned to the superior power of Russia, Austria and Prussia, but, at the same time, the fate of these national revolutions was subordinated to the fate of the proletarian revolution, robbed of its apparent independence, its independence of the great social revolution. The Hungarian shall not be free, nor the Pole, nor the Italian, as long as the worker remains a slave! [40]

Finally, with the victory of the Holy Alliance, Europe took on a form that makes every fresh proletarian upheaval in France directly coincide with a world war. The new French revolution is forced to leave its national soil forthwith and conquer the European terrain, on which alone the revolution of the nineteenth century can be carried through.

Only through the defeat of June, therefore, were all the conditions created under which France can seize the initiative of the European revolution. Only after baptism in the blood of the June insurgents did the tricolor become the flag of the European revolution—the red flag.

And we cry: *The revolution is dead!—Long live the revolution!*

II

FROM JUNE 1848 TO JUNE 13, 1849

(From Number II)

February 25, 1848, had granted the republic to France, June 25 thrust the revolution on her. And revolution, after June, meant: overthrow of bourgeois society, whereas, before February, it had meant overthrow of the form of state.

The June fight had been led by the republican fraction of the bourgeoisie; with victory, the state power inevitably fell to its share. The state of siege laid Paris, gagged, unresisting at its feet, and in the provinces there was a moral state of siege, the threatening, brutal arrogance of the victorious bourgeoisie and the unleashed property fanaticism of the peasants. No danger, therefore, from below!

The smashing of the revolutionary force of the workers simultaneously shattered the political influence of the democratic republicans, *i.e.*, of the republicans in the sense of the petty bourgeoisie, who were represented in the Executive Commission by Ledru-Rollin, in the Constituent National Assembly by the party of the Mountain and in the press by the *Réforme*.[41] Together with the bourgeois republicans they had conspired on April 16 against the proletariat, together with them they had warred against it in the June days. Thus they themselves blasted the background against which their party stood out as a power, for the petty bourgeoisie can only preserve a revolutionary attitude to the bourgeoisie as long as the prolerariat stands behind it. They were dismissed. The sham alliance which the bourgeois republicans, reluctantly and with reservations, concluded with them during the epoch of the Provisional Government and the Executive Commission was openly broken by the bourgeois republicans. Spurned and repulsed as allies, they sank down to subordinate henchmen of the tricolor, from which they could not wring any concessions, but the domination of which they had to support whenever this, and with it the republic, was put in question by the anti-republican bourgeois factions. Finally, these factions, the Orleanists and the Legitimists, found themselves, as a matter of course, in a minority in the Constituent National Assembly. Before the June days, they themselves only dared to react under the mask of bourgeois republicanism; the June victory allowed for a moment the whole of bourgeois France to greet its deliverer in Cavaignac,[42] and when, shortly after the June days, the anti-republicans reconstituted themselves as an independent party, the military dictatorship and the state of siege in Paris permitted it to put out its antennæ only very timidly and bashfully.

Since 1830, the bourgeois republican fraction, with its writers, its speakers, its men of talent and ambition, its deputies, generals, bankers, and lawyers had grouped itself round a Parisian journal, the *National*. In the provinces this journal had its branch newspapers. The coterie of the *National* was the dynasty of the tricolor republic. It immediately took possession of all state offices, of the ministries, the prefecture of police, the post-office management, the positions of prefect, the higher posts of army officers now vacant. At the head of the executive power stood its general, Cavaignac; its editor *en chef*,* Marrast, became permanent president of the Constituent National Assembly. At the same time, as master of ceremonies in his salons, he did the honors of the honest republic.

Even revolutionary French writers awed, as it were, by the republican tradition, have encouraged the mistake that the royalists dominated the Constituent National Assembly. On the contrary, after the June days, the Constituent Assembly remained the exclusive representative of bourgeois republicanism, and it put this face forward all the more decidedly, the more the influence of the tricolor republicans collapsed outside the Assembly. If the question was one of maintaining the form of the bour-

* In chief

geois republic, then the Assembly had the votes of the democratic republicans at its disposal; if one of maintaining the content, then even its mode of speech no longer separated it from the royalist bourgeois factions. For the interests of the bourgeoisie, the material conditions of its class rule and class exploitation, form precisely the content of the bourgeois republic.

Therefore it was not royalism, but bourgeois republicanism which was realized in the life and deeds of this Constituent Assembly, which finally did not die, nor was it killed, but simply decayed.

For the entire duration of its rule, as long as it played the principal and state role on the proscenium, an unbroken sacrificial feast went on in the background—the continual sentencing by courts martial of the imprisoned June insurgents or their deportation without trial. The Constituent Assembly had the tact to admit that in the insurgents of June it was not judging criminals but wiping out enemies.

The first act of the Constituent National Assembly was the setting up of a commission of inquiry into the events of June and of May 15, and into the part played by the socialist and democratic party leaders during these days. The inquiry was directed against Louis Blanc, Ledru-Rollin, and Caussidière. The bourgeois republicans burned with impatience to rid themselves of these rivals. They could have entrusted the venting of their spleen to no more suitable subject than M. Odilon Barrot, the former chief of the dynastic opposition, the incarnation of liberalism, the *nullité grave*,* the profoundly shallow person, who not only had a dynasty to revenge, but even had to settle accounts with the revolutionaries for thwarting his premiership. A sure guarantee of his relentlessness. This Barrot was therefore appointed chairman of the commission of inquiry, and he constructed a complete legal process against the February Revolution, which may be summarized thus: March 17, demonstration; April 16, conspiracy; May 15, attempt; June 23, civil war! Why did he not stretch his erudite researches into criminal law as far back as February 24? The *Journal des Débats* answered:

* Grave nullity.

February 24—that is the foundation of Rome. The origin of states gets lost in a myth, in which one may believe, but which one may not discuss. Louis Blanc and Caussidière were handed over to the courts. The National Assembly completed the work of cleansing itself which it had begun on May 15.

The plan formed by the Provisional Government and again taken up by Goudchaux, of taxing capital—in the form of a mortgage tax—was rejected by the Constituent Assembly; the law that limited the working day to ten hours was repealed; imprisonment for debt was once more introduced; the large section of the French population that can neither read nor write was excluded from the service of juries. Why not from the franchise also? Sureties for journals were again demanded; the right of association was restricted.

But in their haste to give back to the old bourgeois relationships their old guarantees, and to wipe out every trace left behind by the waves of the revolution, the bourgeois republicans came up against an obstacle which threatened them with unexpected danger.

No one had fought more fanatically in the June days for the salvation of property and the restoration of credit than the Parisian petty bourgeois—keepers of cafés and restaurants, *marchands de vins,** small traders, shopkeepers, handicraftsmen, etc. The shopkeeper had pulled himself together and marched against the barricade, in order to restore the traffic which leads from the streets into the shop. But behind the barricade stood the customers and the debtors; before it the creditors of the shop. And when the barricades were thrown down and the workers were crushed and the shopkeepers, drunk with victory, rushed back to their shops, they found the entrance barred by a savior of property, an official agent of credit, who presented them with threatening letters: Overdue bill of exchange! Overdue house rent! Overdue promissory note! Ruined shop! Ruined shopkeeper!

Salvation of property! But the house in which they lived was not their property; the shop which they kept was not their prop-

* Wine merchants.

erty; the commodities in which they dealt were not their property. Neither their business, nor the plate from which they ate, nor the bed on which they slept belonged to them any longer. As against them, precisely this property had to be saved for the house owner, who let the house, for the banker, who discounted the bills of exchange; for the capitalist, who made the advances in cash; for the manufacturer, who entrusted the sale of the commodities to these retailers; for the wholesale dealer, who had credited the raw materials to these handicraftsmen. Restoration of credit! But credit, having regained strength, proved itself a vigorous and jealous god, for it turned the debtor who could not pay from out of his four walls, with wife and child, surrendered his presumed property to capital, and threw the man himself into the debtors' prison, which had once more reared itself threateningly over the corpses of the June insurgents.

The petty bourgeois saw with horror that, by striking down the workers, they had delivered themselves up unresisting into the hands of their creditors. Their bankruptcy, which since February had been dragging on in chronic fashion and had been apparently ignored, was openly declared after June.

Their nominal property had been left unassailed as long as it was of consequence to drive them to the battlefield in the name of property. Now that the great issue with the proletariat had been settled, the small matter of the grocer could in turn be settled. In Paris the mass of liabilities amounted to over 21,-000,000 francs; in the provinces to over 11,000,000. Business tenants of more than 7,000 Paris houses had not paid their rent since February.

While the National Assembly had instituted an inquiry into the political guilt beginning with February, the petty bourgeois, on their part, now demanded an inquiry into the civil debts up to February 24. They assembled *en masse* in the Bourse hall and threateningly demanded on behalf of every dealer who could prove that his bankruptcy was due solely to the stagnation caused by the revolution, and that his business was good on February 24, a lengthening of the terms of payment by judgment of a commercial court and the compelling of the creditor, in consideration of a moderate percentage payment, to liquidate his claim. As a legislative proposal, this question was dealt with in the National Assembly in the form of *concordats à l'amiable*.* The Assembly vacillated; then it suddenly discovered that, at the same time, at Porte St. Denis, thousands of wives and children of the insurgents had prepared an amnesty petition.

In the presence of the resurrected specter of June, the petty bourgeoisie trembled and the National Assembly again retrieved its sternness. The *concordats à l'amiable*, the friendly understanding between creditors and debtors, was rejected in its essential points.

Thus, after the democratic representatives of the petty bourgeois had long been repulsed by the republican representatives of the bourgeoisie within the National Assembly, this parliamentary breach received its civil, real economic meaning, when the petty bourgeois as debtors were handed over to the bourgeois as creditors. A large part of the former were completely ruined and the remainder were only allowed to continue their business under conditions which made them absolute serfs of capital. On August 22, 1848, the National Assembly rejected the *concordats à l'amiable*; on September 19, 1848, in the midst of the state of siege, Prince Louis Bonaparte and the prisoner of Vincennes, the Communist Raspail, were elected as representatives of Paris. The bourgeoisie, however, elected the Jewish money changer and Orleanist, Fould. From all sides at once, therefore, open declaration of war against the Constituent Assembly, against bourgeois republicanism, against Cavaignac.

It needs no argument to show how the mass bankruptcy of the Paris petty bourgeois was bound to produce its effects far beyond its immediate victims, and convulse bourgeois commerce once more, while the state deficit was swollen anew by the costs of the June insurrection, and the state income sank continuously through the hold-up of production, the restricted consumption and the decreasing imports. Cavaignac and the National Assembly could have recourse only to the expedient of a new loan,

* Amicable agreements.

which forced them still further under the yoke of the finance aristocracy.

If the petty bourgeois had harvested bankruptcy and legal liquidation as the fruit of the June victory, the Janissaries * of Cavaignac, the Mobile Guards, found their reward in the soft arms of the courtesans and as "the youthful saviors of society" they received all kinds of homage in the salons of Marrast, the *gentilhomme* of the tricolor, who at the same time served as the Amphitryon † and the troubador of the honest republic. Meanwhile, this social favoritism and the disproportionately higher pay of the Mobile Guard embittered the army, while at the same time all those national illusions vanished with which bourgeois republicanism had been able to attach to itself a part of the army and peasant class under Louis Philippe by means of its journal, the *National*. The role of mediator which Cavaignac and the National Assembly played in North Italy, in order, together with England, to betray it to Austria—this one day of rule destroyed eighteen years of opposition on the part of the *National*. No government was less national than the *National*, none more dependent on England, and, under Louis Philippe, it lived by paraphrasing daily the saying of Cato: *Carthaginem esse delendam:* ‡ none was more servile towards the Holy Alliance, and it had demanded from a Guizot the tearing up of the Treaties of Vienna.[48] The irony of history made Bastide, the ex-editor for foreign affairs of the *National*, the Minister for Foreign Affairs of France, so that he might refute every one of his articles in every one of his dispatches.

For a moment, the army and the peasant class had believed that, simultaneously with the military dictatorship, war abroad and the *gloire* ¶ had been placed on the order of the day in France. But Cavaignac was not the dictatorship of the saber

* Soldiers of the Turkish Guard.
† Host entertainer after the fashion of the hero of Molière's play, *Amphitryon*.
‡ Carthage must be destroyed.
¶ Glory.

over bourgeois society; he was the dictatorship of the bourgeoisie through the saber. And of the soldier they now required
only the gendarme. Cavaignac concealed under the stern features of old republican resignation humdrum submission to the
humiliating conditions of his bourgeois office. *L'argent n'a pas
de maître!* Money has no master! He idealized this old election
cry of the *tiers-état* * as, in general, the Constituent Assembly
did, by translating it into political speech: The bourgeoisie has
no king; the true form of its rule is the republic.

And the "great organic work" of the Constituent National
Assembly consisted in working out this form, in producing a
republican constitution. The re-christening of the Christian cal-
endar as a republican one, of the saintly Bartholomew as the
saintly Robespierre made no more change in the wind and
weather than this constitution made or was intended to make in
bourgeois society. Where it went beyond the change of costume,
it put on record the existing facts. Thus it solemnly registered
the fact of the republic, the fact of universal suffrage, the fact of
a single sovereign National Assembly in place of two limited
constitutional chambers. Thus it registered and regulated the
fact of the dictatorship of Cavaignac by replacing the stationary,
irresponsible hereditary monarchy with itinerant, responsible,
electoral monarchy, with a quadrennial presidency. Thus, no
less, it elevated to a constitutional law the fact of the extraordinary powers with which the National Assembly, after the shock
of May 15 and June 25, had providently invested its president
in the interest of its own security. The remainder of the constitution was a work of terminology. The royalist labels were
torn off the machine of the old monarchy and republican labels
were stuck on. Marrast, former editor-in-chief of the *National*,
now editor *en chef* of the constitution, acquitted himself of this
academic task not without talent.

The Constituent Assembly resembled that Chilian official who
wanted to regulate property relations in land more firmly by
a cadastral survey, just at the moment when subterranean rum-
blings had already announced the volcanic eruption that was

* Third estate.

to hurl away the land itself from under his feet. While in theory it accurately measured the forms in which the rule of the bourgeoisie found republican expression, in reality it held its own only by the suspension of all formulas, by force *sans phrase*,* by the state of siege. Two days before it began its work on the constitution, it proclaimed its permanency. Formerly, constitutions had been made and adopted as soon as the social process of revolution had reached a point of rest, the newly formed class relationships had established themselves and the contending factions of the ruling class had recourse to a compromise which allowed them to continue the struggle between themselves and at the same time to keep the exhausted masses of the people out of it. On the other hand, this constitution did not sanction any social revolution; it sanctioned the momentary victory of the old society over the revolution.

The first draft of the constitution, made before the June days, still contained the *droit au travail*, the right to work, the first clumsy formula wherein the revolutionary aspirations of the proletariat are summarized. It was transformed into the *droit à l'assistance*, the right to public relief, and what modern state does not feed its paupers in some form or other? The right to work is, in the bourgeois sense, an absurdity, a miserable, pious wish. But behind the right to work stands the power over capital; behind the power over capital the appropriation of the means of production, their subjection to the associated working class and, therefore, the abolition of wage labor as well as of capital and of their mutual relationships. Behind the "right to work" stood the June insurrection. The Constituent Assembly, which set the revolutionary proletariat factually *hors la loi*, outside the law, had on principle to throw the formula out of the constitution, the law of laws, had to pronounce its anathema on the "right to work." But it did not stop there. As Plato banned the poets from his republic, so it banished forever from its republic—the progressive tax. But the progressive tax is not only a bourgeois measure, which can be carried out within the existing relations of production to a

* Without circumlocution.

greater or less degree; it was the only means of binding the middle strata of bourgeois society to the *honnête* † republic, of reducing the state debt, of holding in check the anti-republican majority of the bourgeoisie.

In the matter of the *concordats à l'amiable*, tricolor republicans had actually sacrificed the petty bourgeoisie to the big bourgeoisie. They elevated this isolated fact to a principle by the legal prohibition of the progressive tax. They put bourgeois reform on the same level as proletarian revolution. But what class then remained as the mainstay of their republic? The big bourgeoisie. And its mass was anti-republican. If it exploited the republicans of the *National* in order to re-establish the old relations of economic life, it thought, on the other hand, of exploiting the re-established social relations in order to restore the political reforms that corresponded to them. Even at the beginning of October, Cavaignac saw himself forced to make Dufaure and Vivien, previously ministers of Louis Philippe, ministers of the republic, however much the brainless Puritans of his own party growled and blustered.

While the tricolor constitution rejected every compromise with the petty bourgeoisie and did not know how to attach any new social element to the new state form, it hastened, on the other hand, to give back to a body that constituted the most hardbitten and fanatical defender of the old state, its traditional immunity. It raised the irremovability of judges, which had been questioned by the Provisional Government, to a constitutional law. The one king whom it had removed rose again multiplied in these irremovable inquisitors of legality.

The French press has analyzed from numerous aspects the contradictions of M. Marrast's constitution, for example, the co-existence of two sovereigns, the National Assembly and the President, etc., etc.

The most comprehensive contradiction of this constitution, however, consisted in the following: The classes whose social slavery the constitution is to perpetuate, proletariat, peasants, petty bourgeois, it puts in possession of political power through

† Honest.

universal suffrage. And from the class whose old social power it sanctions, the bourgeoisie, it withdraws the political guarantees of this power. It forces its political rule into democratic conditions, which at every moment help the hostile classes to victory and jeopardize the very foundations of bourgeois society. From the former classes it demands that they should not go forward from political to social emancipation; from the others that they should not go back from social to political restoration.

These contradictions perturbed the bourgeois republicans very little. To the same extent as they ceased to be indispensable— they were indispensable only as the advance fighters of the old society against the revolutionary proletariat—a few weeks after their victory they fell from the position of a party to that of a coterie. And they treated the constitution as a big intrigue. Above all, what should be constituted in it was the rule of the coterie. The President should be a protracted Cavaignac; the Legislative Assembly a protracted Constituent Assembly. They hoped to reduce the political power of the masses of the people to a fictitious power, and to be able to make sufficient play with this sham power itself, continually to keep hanging over the majority of the bourgeoisie the dilemma of the June days: realm of the *National*, or realm of anarchy.

The work on the constitution, which was begun on September 4, was ended on October 23. On September 2 the Constituent Assembly had decided not to dissolve until the organic laws supplementing the constitution were enacted. None the less, it decided to call into being the creation, most of all its own, the President, on December 4, long before the circle of its own activity was closed. So sure it was of hailing in the *homunculus* * of the constitution, the son of his mother. As a precaution it was provided that, if none of the candidates received two million votes, the election should pass over from the nation to the Constituent Assembly.

Fruitless provisions! The first day of the realization of the constitution was the last day of the rule of the Constituent As-

* According to Paracelsus, a diminutive man produced artificially, and hence endowed with magic powers.

sembly. At the bottom of the ballot box lay its sentence of death. It sought the "son of his mother" and found "the nephew of his uncle." Saul Cavaignac obtained one million votes, but David Napoleon obtained six million. Saul Cavaignac was defeated six times over.

December 10, 1848, was the day of the peasant insurrection. Only from this day does the February of the French peasants date. The symbol that expressed their entry into the revolutionary movement, clumsily cunning, knavishly naïve, doltishly sublime, a calculated superstition, a pathetic burlesque, a cleverly stupid anachronism, a world historical piece of buffoonery and an undecipherable hieroglyphic for the understanding of the civilized—this symbol bore the unmistakable features of the class that represents barbarism within civilization. The republic had announced itself to this class with the tax collector; it announced itself to the republic with the emperor. Napoleon was the only man who had exhaustively represented the interests and the imagination of the peasant class, newly created in 1789. By writing his name on the front page of the republic, it declared war abroad and the enforcing of its class interests at home. Napoleon, for the peasants, was not a person but a program. With banners, with beat of drums and blare of trumpets, they marched to the polling booths shouting: *plus d'impôts, à bas les riches, à bas la république, vive l'Empereur.* No more taxes, down with the rich, down with the republic, long live the emperor! Behind the emperor was hidden the peasant war. The republic that they voted down was the republic of the rich.

December 10 was the *coup d'état* of the peasants, which overthrew the existing government. And from that day on, when they had taken a government from France and given one to her, their eyes were turned steadily on Paris. For a moment active heroes of the revolutionary drama, they could no longer be forced back into the passive and spineless role of the chorus.

The other classes helped to complete the election victory of the peasants. The election of Napoleon, for the proletariat, meant the deposition of Cavaignac, the overthrow of the Constituent Assembly, the dismissal of bourgeois republicanism, the rescinding of the June victory. For the petty bourgeoisie, Napoleon meant the rule of the debtors over the creditors. For the majority of the big bourgeoisie the election of Napoleon meant an open breach with the fraction of which it had had to make use, for a moment, against the revolution, but which became intolerable to it as soon as this fraction sought to consolidate the position of the moment into the constitutional position. Napoleon in place of Cavaignac, for the majority of the big bourgeoisie, meant the monarchy in place of the republic, the beginning of the royalist restoration, a shy hint at Orleans, the lily hidden beneath the violet.[44] Finally, the army voted for Napoleon against the Mobile Guard, against the peace idyll, for war.

Thus it happened, as the *Neue Rheinische Zeitung* stated, that the most simple-minded man in France acquired the most multifarious significance. Just because he was nothing, he could signify everything save himself. Meanwhile, different as the meaning of the name Napoleon might be in the mouths of the different classes, with this name each wrote in its bulletin: Down with the party of the *National*, down with Cavaignac, down with the Constituent Assembly, down with the bourgeois republic. The Minister, Dufaure, publicly declared in the Constituent Assembly: December 10 is a second February 24.

Petty bourgeoisie and proletariat had voted *en bloc* * for Napoleon, in order to vote against Cavaignac and, by pooling their votes, to wrest the final decision from the Constituent Assembly. The more advanced sections of the two classes, however, put forward their own candidates. Napoleon was the collective name of all parties in coalition against the bourgeois republic, Ledru-Rollin and Raspail were the proper names, the former of the democratic petty bourgeoisie, the latter of the revolutionary proletariat. The votes for Raspail, the proletarians and their socialist spokesmen loudly declared, were to be merely a demonstration, so many protests against either presidency, *i.e.*, against the constitution itself, so many votes against Ledru-Rollin, the first act by which the proletariat, as an independent

* In a mass.

political party, cut loose from the democratic party. This party, on the other hand, the democratic petty bourgeoisie and its parliamentary representative, the Mountain, treated the candidature of Ledru-Rollin with all the seriousness with which they are in the habit of solemnly duping themselves. For the rest, this was their last attempt, as against the proletariat, to set themselves up as an independent party. Not only the republican bourgeois party, but also the democratic bourgeoisie and its Mountain were beaten on December 10.

France now possessed a Napoleon side by side with a Mountain, proof that both were only the lifeless caricatures of the great realities whose names they bore. Louis Napoleon, with the emperor's hat and the eagle, parodied the old Napoleon no more miserably than the Mountain, with its phrases borrowed from 1793 and its demagogic poses, parodied the old Mountain. Thus the traditional superstition in 1793 was stripped off at the same time as the traditional superstition in Napoleon. The revolution had only come into its own when it had won its own original name and it could only do that when the modern revolutionary class, the industrial proletariat, came dominatingly into its foreground. One can say that December 10 dumbfounded the Mountain and caused it to grow confused in its own mind, because it laughingly cut short the classical analogy to the old revolution with a rude peasant joke.

On December 20 Cavaignac laid down his office and the Constituent Assembly proclaimed Louis Napoleon President of the republic. On December 19, the last day of its autocracy, it rejected the proposal for amnesty for the June insurgents. To revoke the decree of June 27, through which it had condemned 15,000 insurgents to deportation by evading legal judgment, did not that mean to revoke the June battle itself?

Odilon Barrot, the last Minister of Louis Philippe, became the first Minister of Louis Napoleon. Just as Louis Napoleon dated his rule, not from December 10, but from a decree of the Senate of 1806, so he found a prime minister who did not date his ministry from December 20, but from a royal decree of February 24. As the legitimate heir of Louis Philippe, Louis

Napoleon softened the change of government by retaining the old ministry, which, moreover, had not had time to wear itself out, since it had not found time to come to life.

The chiefs of the royalist bourgeois factions advised him in this choice. The head of the old dynastic opposition, who had unconsciously made the transition to the republicans of the *National*, was still more fitted to make with full consciousness the transition from the bourgeois republic to the monarchy.

Odilon Barrot was the head of the one old opposition party which, always fruitlessly struggling for ministerial portfolios, had not yet worn itself out. In rapid succession the revolution threw all the old opposition parties to the top of the state, so that they had to deny and revoke their old phrases not only in deeds but in words, and might finally be flung all together, combined in a repulsive mixture, on the dung heap of history by the people. And this Barrot was spared no apostasy, this incarnation of bourgeois liberalism, who for eighteen years had hidden the rascally vacuity of his mind behind the serious demeanor of his body. If, at certain moments, the far too striking contrast between the thistles of the present and the laurels of the past startled the man himself, a glance in the mirror gave back his ministerial serenity and human self-admiration. What beamed at him from the mirror was Guizot, whom he had always envied, who had always mastered him, Guizot himself, but Guizot with the Olympian forehead of Odilon. What he overlooked were the ears of Midas.[45]

The Barrot of February 24 first became manifest in the Barrot of December 20. Associated with him, the Orleanist and Voltairian was the Legitimist and Jesuit, Falloux, as Minister for Education.

A few days later, the Ministry for Home Affairs was given to Leon Faucher, the Malthusian. Law, religion and political economy! The ministry of Barrot contained all this and, in addition, a combination of Orleanists and Legitimists. Only the Bonapartist was lacking. Bonaparte still hid his longing to signify Napoleon, for Soulouque did not yet play Toussaint l'Ouverture.[46]

The party of the *National* was immediately relieved of all the higher posts where it had dug itself in. The positions of Prefect of Police, Director of the Post, Procurator General, Mayor of Paris, were all filled by old creatures of the monarchy. Changarnier, the Legitimist, received the unified supreme command of the National Guard of the Department of the Seine, the Mobile Guard and the troops of the first military division; Bugeaud, the Orleanist, was nominated as the commander-in-chief of the Alpine army. This change of officials continued uninterruptedly under the Barrot government. The first act of his ministry was the restoration of the old royalist administration. The official scene was transformed in a trice— scenery, costumes, speech, actors, supers, dummies, prompters, the position of the parties, the theme of the drama, the content of the conflict, the whole situation. Only the antediluvian Constituent Assembly remained in its place. But from the hour when the National Assembly had installed Bonaparte, Bonaparte Barrot and Barrot Changarnier, France stepped out of the period of the constituted republic. And in the constituted republic what place was there for a Constituent Assembly? After the earth had been created, there was nothing else for its creator to do but to take flight to heaven. The Constituent Assembly was determined not to follow his example; the National Assembly was the last asylum for the party of the bourgeois republicans. If all levers of executive power had been wrested from it, was there not left to it constituent omnipotence? Its first thought was to hold under all circumstances the positions of sovereignty that it occupied, and thence to reconquer the lost ground. The Barrot ministry once displaced by a ministry of the *National*, and the royalist personnel would have to vacate the palaces of the administration forthwith and the tricolor personnel would move in again triumphantly. The National Assembly resolved on the overthrow of the ministry and the ministry itself offered an opportunity for the attack, than which the Constituent Assembly could not have found a better.

It must be remembered that for the peasants Louis Bonaparte signified: No more taxes! He sat for six days in the President's chair, and on the seventh day, on December 27, his ministry proposed the retention of the salt tax, the abolition of which the Provisional Government had decreed. The salt tax shares with the wine tax the privilege of being the scapegoat of the old French financial system, particularly in the eyes of the country folk. The Barrot ministry could not have put into the mouth of the elect of the peasants any more mordant epigram on his electors than the words: Restoration of the salt tax! With the salt tax, Bonaparte lost his revolutionary salt—the Napoleon of the peasant insurrection dissolved like an apparition, and nothing remained but the great unknown of royalist bourgeois intrigue. And not without intention, the Barrot ministry made this act of tactlessly rude disillusionment the first governmental act of the President.

The Constituent Assembly, on its part, seized eagerly on the double opportunity of overthrowing the ministry, and, as against the elect of the peasantry, of setting itself up as the representative of peasant interests. It rejected the proposal of the finance minister, reduced the salt tax to a third of its former amount, thus increased by six millions a state deficit of five hundred and sixty millions, and, after this vote of no confidence, calmly awaited the resignation of the ministry. So little did it comprehend the new world that surrounded it and its own changed position. Behind the ministry stood the President and behind the President stood six millions, who had placed in the ballot box as many votes of no confidence in the Constituent Assembly. The Constituent Assembly gave the nation back its no confidence vote. Absurd exchange! It forgot that its votes had lost compulsory quotation. The rejection of the salt tax only matured the decision of Bonaparte and his ministry to "end" the Constituent Assembly. That long duel began which lasted half the entire life of the Constituent Assembly. January 29, March 31 and May 3 are the *journées*, the great days of this crisis, just so many forerunners of June 13.

Frenchmen, for example, Louis Blanc, have construed January 29 as the date of the emergence of a constitutional contradiction, the contradiction between a sovereign, indissoluble National

Assembly born of universal suffrage and a President, who, in words, was responsible to the Assembly, but who, in reality, was not only similarly sanctioned by universal suffrage and, in addition, united in his own person all the votes that were split up a hundred times and distributed among the individual members of the National Assembly, but was also in full possession of the whole executive power, above which the National Assembly hovered as a merely moral force. This interpretation of January 29 confounds the language of the struggle on the platform, through the press and in the clubs, with its real content. Louis Bonaparte as against the National Assembly—that was not a one-sided constitutional power as against another; it was not the executive power as against the legislative, it was the constituted bourgeois republic itself as against the instruments of its constitution, as against the honors-seeking intrigues and ideological demands of the revolutionary bourgeois faction that had founded it and was now amazed to find that its constituted republic looked like a restored monarchy, and now violently desired to adhere to the constituting period with its conditions, its illusions, its language and its personnel and to prevent the mature bourgeois republic from emerging in its complete and peculiar form. As the Constituent National Assembly represented Cavaignac who had fallen back into it, so Bonaparte represented the Legislative National Assembly, that had not yet been estranged from him, *i.e.*, the National Assembly of the constituted bourgeois republic.

The election of Bonaparte could only become explicable by putting in the place of the one name its many-sided significance, by repeating itself in the election of the new National Assembly. The mandate of the old was annulled by December 10. On January 29, therefore, it was not the President and the National Assembly of the same republic that were face to face, it was the National Assembly of the republic in the making and the President of the republic in being, two powers that embodied quite different periods in the life process of the republic; the one the small republican section of the bourgeoisie that alone could proclaim the republic, wrest it from the revolutionary proletariat by street fighting and a reign of terror, and draft its ideal features in the constitution, and the other the whole royalist mass of the bourgeoisie that alone could rule in this constituted bourgeois republic, strip the constitution of its ideological trimmings, and realize by its legislation and administration the indispensable conditions for the subjection of the proletariat.

The storm which broke on January 29 gathered its elements together during the whole month of January. The Constituent Assembly wanted to drive the Barrot ministry to resign by its no confidence vote. The Barrot ministry, on the other hand, proposed that the Constituent Assembly should give itself a definitive no-confidence vote, decide on suicide and decree its own dissolution. Rateau, one of the most obscure deputies, at the order of the ministry, on January 6 brought this motion before the Constituent Assembly, the same Constituent Assembly that already in August had resolved not to dissolve until a whole series of organic laws supplementing the constitution had been enacted. Fould, the ministerialist, bluntly declared to it that its dissolution was necessary "for the restoration of the deranged credit." And did it not derange credit when it prolonged the provisional stage and, with Barrot, again called Bonaparte in question, and, with Bonaparte, the constituted republic? Barrot, the Olympian, became a raving Roland with the prospect of seeing the finally grabbed premiership, which the republicans had already withheld from him once for a decade, *i.e.*, for ten months, again torn from him after scarcely two weeks' enjoyment of it—Barrot confronting his wretched Assembly, outtyrannized the tyrant. His mildest words were "no future is possible with it." And actually it did only represent the past. "It is incapable," he added ironically, "of surrounding the republic with the institutions which are necessary for its consolidation." Incapable indeed! With its exclusive antagonism to the proletariat, its bourgeois energy was simultaneously broken, and with its antagonism to the royalists its republican exuberance lived anew. Thus it was doubly incapable of consolidating the bourgeois republic, which it no longer comprehended, by means of the corresponding institutions.

Simultaneously with Rateau's motion the ministry evoked a storm of petitions throughout the land, and from all corners of France came flying daily at the head of the Constituent Assembly bundles of *billets doux* * in which it was more or less categorically requested to dissolve and make its will. The Constituent Assembly, on its side, called forth counter petitions, in which it caused itself to be requested to remain alive. The election struggle between Bonaparte and Cavaignac was renewed as a petition struggle for or against the dissolution of the National Assembly. The petitions were to be subsequent commentaries on December 10. During the whole of January the agitation continued.

In the conflict between the Constituent Assembly and the President, the former could not go back to the general election as its origin, for the appeal was from it to universal suffrage. It could base itself on no regular power for the issue was the struggle against the legal power. It could not overthrow the ministry by no-confidence votes, as it again essayed to do on January 6 and 26, for the ministry did not ask for its confidence. Only one possibility was left to it, that of insurrection. The fighting forces of the insurrection were the republican part of the National Guard, the Mobile Guard and the centers of the revolutionary proletariat, the clubs. The Mobile Guards, those heroes of the June days, in December as well formed the organized fighting force of the republican bourgeois factions, just as before June the National *Ateliers* had formed the organized fighting force of the revolutionary proletariat. As the Executive Commission of the Constituent Assembly directed its brutal attack on the National *Ateliers,* when it had to put an end to the pretensions of the proletariat that had become unbearable, so the ministry of Bonaparte directed its attack on the Mobile Guard, when it had to put an end to the pretensions of the republican bourgeois factions that had become unbearable. It ordered the dissolution of the Mobile Guard. One half of it was dismissed and thrown on the street, the other was organized on monarchist instead of democratic lines, and its pay was re-

* Love letters.

duced to the usual pay of troops of the line. The Mobile Guard
found itself in the position of the June insurgents and every day
the press carried public confessions in which it admitted its
blame for June and implored the proletariat for forgiveness.
And the clubs? From the moment when the Constituent Assembly called the President in question in the person of Barrot,
and the constituted bourgeois republic in the person of the
President, and the bourgeois republic in general in the person of
the constituted republic, all the constituent elements of the
February republic necessarily ranged themselves round it, all
the parties that wished to overthrow the existing republic and,
by violent retrograde process to reshape it to the republic of
their class interests and principles. What was done was again
undone, the crystallizations of the revolutionary movement had
again become fluid, the republic that the parties fought for was
again the indefinite republic of the February days, the defining
of which each party reserved for itself. For a moment the
parties again took up their old February positions, without shar-
ing the illusions of February. The tricolor republicans of the
National again leant on the democratic republicans of the
Réforme and pushed them into the foreground of the parliamentary struggle as advance fighters. The democratic republicans again leant on the socialist republicans—on January 27
a public manifesto announced their reconcilation and alliance—
and prepared their insurrectional background in the clubs. The
ministerial press treated the tricolor republicans correctly as the
resurrected insurgents of June. In order to maintain itself at
the head of the bourgeois republic, it called in question the
bourgeois republic itself. On January 26 the minister, Faucher,
proposed a law on the right of association, the first paragraph
of which read: "the clubs are forbidden." He moved that this
bill should immediately be discussed as urgent. The Constituent
Assembly rejected the motion of urgency, and on January 27
Ledru-Rollin put forward a proposition, with 230 signatures
appended to it, impeaching the ministry for violation of the constitution. The impeachment of the ministry at a moment when
such an act was a tactless disclosure of the impotence of the

judge, to wit, the majority of the Chamber, or was an impotent protest of the accuser against this majority itself—that was the great revolutionary trump that the latter day Mountain played from now on at each high spot of the crisis. Poor Mountain! crushed by the weight of its own name.

On May 15, Blanqui, Barbès, Raspail, etc., had attempted to break up the Constituent Assembly by forcing an entrance into its meeting hall at the head of the Paris proletariat. Barrot prepared a moral May 15 for the same Assembly when he wanted to dictate its self-dissolution and close the hall. The same Assembly had commissioned Barrot with the official inquiry against the May accused, and now at the moment when he appeared before it like a royalist Blanqui, when it sought for allies against him in the clubs, among the revolutionary proletarians, in the party of Blanqui—at this moment the relentless Barrot tormented it with the proposal to withdraw the May prisoners from the Court of Assizes and hand them over to the High Court, to the *haute cour*, devised by the party of the *National*. Remarkable how the fear excited for a ministerial portfolio could pound out of the head of a Barrot points worthy of a Beaumarchais! [47] The National Assembly, after much vacillation, accepted his proposal. As against the makers of the May attempt, it reverted to its normal character.

If the Constituent Assembly was driven to insurrection against the President and the ministers, the President and the ministers were driven to a *coup d'état* against the Constituent Assembly, for they had no legal means of dissolving it. But the Constituent Assembly was the mother of the constitution and the constitution was the mother of the President. With the *coup d'état*, the President tore up the constitution and extinguished his republican lawful title. He was then forced to pull out the imperial lawful title; but the imperial lawful title woke up the Orleanist lawful title and both paled before the Legitimist lawful title. The downfall of the legal republic could only then throw to the top its most extreme opposite pole, the Legitimist monarchy, at a moment when the Orleanist party was still only the vanquished of February and Bonaparte was still only the victor of

December 10, when both could still only oppose to republican usurpation their likewise usurped monarchist titles. The legitimists were aware of the favorableness of the moment; they conspired openly. They could hope to find their Monk[48] in General Changarnier. The accession of the White monarchy was as openly predicted in their clubs as was that of the Red republic in the proletarian clubs.

The ministry would have escaped all difficulties through a happily suppressed rising. "Legality is the death of us," cried Odilon Barrot. A rising would have allowed it, under the pretext of the *salut public*,* to dissolve the Constituent Assembly, to violate the constitution in the interests of the constitution itself. The brutal action of Odilon Barrot in the National Assembly, the motion for the dissolution of the clubs, the tumultuous removal of 30 tricolor prefects, and their replacement by royalists, the dissolution of the Mobile Guard, the ill treatment of their chiefs by Changarnier, the reinstatement of L'Herminier, the professor who was impossible even under Guizot, the toleration of the Legitimist boasting—all these were just so many provocations to mutiny. But the mutiny remained mute. It expected its signal from the Constituent Assembly and not from the ministry.

Finally came January 29, the day on which the decision was to be taken on the motion of Mathieu (*de la Drôme*) for unconditional rejection of Rateau's motion. Legitimists, Orleanists, Bonapartists, the Mobile Guard, the Mountain, the clubs, all conspired on this day, each just as much against ostensible allies as against ostensible enemies. Bonaparte, mounted on horseback, mustered a part of the troop on the *Place de la Concorde;* Changarnier play-acted with a display of strategic maneuvers; the Constituent Assembly found its building occupied by the military. This Assembly, the center of all the conflicting hopes, fears, expectations, ferments, tensions and conspiracies, this lionhearted Assembly, did not falter for a moment, when it came nearer to the world spirit than usual. It was like that fighter who not only feared the use of his own weapons, but also felt

* Public safety.

himself obliged to maintain the weapons of his opponent unimpaired. Scorning death, it signed its own death warrant, and rejected the unconditional rejection of the Rateau motion.[49] Even in the state of siege, it set limits to a constituent activity whose necessary frame had been the state of siege of Paris. It revenged itself worthily, when, on the following day, it instituted an inquiry into the fright that the ministry had given it on January 29. The Mountain showed its lack of revolutionary energy and political understanding by allowing itself to be used by the party of the *National* in this great comedy of intrigues as the crier in the contest. The party of the *National* had made its last attempt to maintain, in the constituted republic, the monopoly of rule that it had possessed during the formative period of the bourgeois republic. It was shipwrecked.

While in the January crisis it was a question of the existence of the Constituent Assembly, in the crisis of March 21, it was a question of the existence of the constitution—there of the personnel of the National Party, here of its ideal. There is no need to point out that the honest republicans surrendered the exaltation of their ideology more cheaply than the worldly enjoyment of governmental power.

On March 21 there was on the order of the day in the National Assembly Faucher's bill against the right of association: the suppression of the clubs. Article 8 of the constitution guarantees to all Frenchmen the right to associate. The prohibition of the clubs was, therefore, an evident violation of the constitution, and the Constituent Assembly itself had to canonize the profanation of its holies. But the clubs—these were the gathering points, the conspiratorial seats of the revolutionary proletariat. The National Assembly had itself forbidden the coalition of the workers against their bourgeois. And the clubs—what were they but a coalition of the whole working class against the whole bourgeois class, the formation of a workers' state against the bourgeois state? Were they not just so many constituent assemblies of the proletariat and just so many military detachments of revolt in fighting trim? What the constitution was above all to constitute was the rule of the bourgeoisie. The constitution, therefore, could manifestly only understand by the right of association the associations that harmonized with the rule of the bourgeoisie, *i.e.*, with the bourgeois order. If, for reasons of theoretical propriety, it expressed itself in general terms, was not the government and the National Assembly there to interpret and apply it in a given case? And if in the primitive epoch of the republic, the clubs actually were forbidden by the state of siege, had they not also to be forbidden in the ordered, constituted republic by the law? The tricolor republicans had nothing to oppose to this prosaic interpretation of the constitution but the high-flown phraseology of the constitution. A section of them, Pagnerre, Duclerc, etc., voted for the ministry and thereby gave it a majority. The others, with the archangel, Cavaignac, and the father of the church, Marrast, at their head, after the article on the prohibition of the clubs had gone through, retired to a special committee room in conjunction with Ledru-Rollin and the Mountain—"and held a council." The National Assembly was paralyzed; it had no longer a quorum. At the right time, M. Cremieux remembered in the committee room that the way from here led directly to the street and that it was no longer February 1848, but March 1849. The party of the *National*, suddenly enlightened, returned to the National Assembly's hall of session, behind it the Mountain, duped once more. The latter, constantly tormented by revolutionary longings, just as constantly clutched at constitutional possibilities, and always felt itself more in place behind the bourgeois republicans than in front of the revolutionary proletariat. Thus the comedy was played. And the Constituent Assembly itself had decreed that the violation of the letter of the constitution was the only appropriate realization of its spirit.

There was only one point left to settle, the relation of the constituted republic to the European revolution, its foreign policy. On May 8, 1849, an unwonted excitement prevailed in the Constitutional Assembly, whose term of life was due to end in a few days. The attack of the French army on Rome, its repulse by the Romans, its political infamy and military disgrace, the assassination of the Roman republic by the French republic, the first Italian campaign of the second Napoleon was on the order of the day. The Mountain had once more played its great trump, Ledru-Rollin had laid on the President's table the inevitable bill of impeachment against the ministry and this time also against Bonaparte for violation of the constitution.

The motive of May 8 repeated itself later as the motive of June 13. Let us get clear about the expedition to Rome.

In the middle of November 1848, Cavaignac had already sent a battle fleet to Civita Vecchia, in order to protect the Pope, to take him on board and to ship him over to France. The Pope was to bless the honest republic, and to ensure the election of Cavaignac as President. With the Pope, Cavaignac wanted to angle for the priests, with the priests for the peasants, and with the peasants for the Presidency. The expedition of Cavaignac, an election advertisement in its immediate purpose, was at the same time a protest and a threat against the Roman revolution. It contained in embryo France's intervention in favor of the Pope.

This intervention against the Roman republic, on the Pope's behalf, in association with Austria and Naples, was decided on at the first meeting of Bonaparte's ministerial council on December 23. Falloux in the ministry, that meant the Pope in Rome and in the Rome—of the Pope. Bonaparte did not need the Pope any longer in order to become the President of the peasants; but he needed the conservation of the Pope, in order to conserve the peasants of the President. Their credulity had made him President. With faith they lost credulity, and with the Pope, faith. And the Orleanists and Legitimists in coalition, who ruled in Bonaparte's name! Before the king was restored, the power had to be restored that consecrates kings. Apart from their royalism: without the old Rome, subject to his worldly rule, no Pope; without the Pope, no catholicism; without catholicism, no French religion; and without religion, what became of the old French society? The mortgage that the peasant has on heavenly blessings guarantees the mortgage that the bourgeois has on peasant lands. The Roman revolution was, therefore, an attack on property, on the bourgeois order, dreadful as the June revolution. Re-established bourgeois rule in France re-

quired the restoration of papist rule in Rome. Finally, to smite
the Roman revolutionaries was to smite the allies of the French
revolutionaries; the alliance of the counter-revolutionary classes
in the constituted French republic was necessarily supplemented
by the alliance of the French republic with the Holy Alliance,
with Naples and Austria. The decision of the ministerial council
of December 23 was no secret for the Constituent Assembly. On
January 8 Ledru-Rollin had already interrogated the ministry
concerning it; the ministry had denied it and the National Assembly had proceeded to the order of the day. Did it trust the
word of the ministry? We know that it spent the whole month
of January in giving the ministry no-confidence votes. But if it
was part of the ministry's role to lie, it was part of the National
Assembly's role to feign belief in its lie and thereby save the
republican *déhors*.*

Meanwhile, Piedmont was beaten, King Albert had abdicated and the Austrian army knocked at the door of France.
Ledru-Rollin vehemently interrogated. The ministry proved
that it had only continued in North Italy the policy of Cavaignac, and Cavaignac only the policy of the Provisional
Government, *i.e.*, of Ledru-Rollin. This time it even reaped a
vote of confidence from the National Assembly and was authorized to occupy temporarily a suitable point in Upper Italy, in
order to give support to peaceful negotiations with Austria concerning the integrity of Sardinian territory and the question of
Rome. It is well known that the fate of Italy is decided on the
battlefields of North Italy. Hence Rome had fallen with Lom-
bardy and Piedmont, or France had to declare war on Austria
and thereby on the European counter-revolution. Did the National Assembly suddenly take the Barrot ministry for the old
Committee of Public Safety? Or itself for the Convention? Why,
then, the military occupation of a point in Upper Italy? The
expedition against Rome was covered with this transparent veil.

On April 14, 14,000 men sailed under Oudinot for Civita
Vecchia; on April 16, the National Assembly voted the ministry
a credit of 1,200,000 francs for the maintenance of a fleet of

* Appearances.

intervention in the Mediterranean Sea for three months. Thus it gave the ministry every means of intervening against Rome, while it adopted the pose of letting it intervene against Austria. It did not see what the ministry did; it only heard what it said. Such faith was not found in Israel; the Constituent Assembly had fallen into the position of not daring to know what the constituted republic had to do.

Finally, on May 8, the last scene of the comedy was played; the Constituent Assembly urged the ministry to take swift measures to bring the Italian expedition back to the aim set for it. Bonaparte that same evening inserted a letter in the *Moniteur*, in which he lavished the greatest appreciation on Oudinot. On May 11, the National Assembly rejected the bill of impeachment against this same Bonaparte and his ministry. And the Mountain, which, instead of tearing this web of deceit to pieces, took the parliamentary comedy tragically, in order itself to play in it the role of Fouquier-Tinville,[50] did it not reveal its natural petty-bourgeois calf's hide under the borrowed lion's skin of the Convention!

The last half of the life of the Constituent Assembly is summarized thus: On January 29, it admits that the royalist bourgeois factions are the natural superiors of the republic constituted by it; on March 21, that the violation of the constitution is its realization, and on May 11, that the passive alliance of the French republic, bombastically proclaimed, with the struggling peoples means its active alliance with the European counter-revolution.

This miserable Assembly left the stage, after it had given itself the pleasure, two days before the anniversary of its birthday, May 4, of rejecting the motion of amnesty for the June insurgents. Its power shattered, held in deadly hatred by the people, repulsed, maltreated, contemptuously thrown aside by the bourgeoisie, whose tool it was, forced in the second half of its life to disavow the first, robbed of its republican illusion, without great creations in the past, without hope in the future and with its living body dying bit by bit, it knew how to gal-vanize its own corpse only by continually recalling and living through over again the June victory, substantiating itself by constantly repeated damnation of the damned. Vampire, that lived on the blood of the June insurgents!

It left behind the state deficit, increased by the costs of the June insurrection, by the loss of the salt tax, by the compensation it paid the plantation owners for abolishing Negro slavery, by the costs of the Roman expedition, by the loss of the wine tax, the abolition of which it resolved on when lying at its last gasp, a malicious old man, happy to impose on his laughing heir a compromising debt of honor.

With the beginning of March the agitation for the election of the Legislative National Assembly had commenced. Two main groups opposed each other, the party of order ,and the democratic-socialist or Red party; between the two stood the *Friends of the Constitution*, under which name the tricolor republicans of the *National* sought to put forward a party. The party of order was formed directly after the June days; only after December 10 had allowed it to cast off the coterie of the *National*, of the bourgeois republicans, did it disclose the secret of its existence, the coalition of Orleanists and Legitimists into one party. The bourgeois class fell apart into two big factions, which, alternately, the big landed proprietors under the restored monarchy and the finance aristocracy and the industrial bourgeoisie under the July monarchy, had maintained a monopoly of power. Bourbon was the royal name for the predominant influence of the interests of the one faction, Orleans the royal name for the predominant influence of the interests of the other faction—the nameless realm of the republic was the only one in which both factions could maintain in equal power the common class interest, without giving up their mutual rivalry. If the bourgeois republic could not be anything but the perfected and clearly expressed rule of the whole bourgeois class, could it be anything but the rule of the Orleanists supplemented by the Legitimists, and of the Legitimists supplemented by the Orleanists, the synthesis of the restoration and the July monarchy? The bourgeois republicans of the *National* did not represent any large fraction of their class resting on economic foundations.

They had only the importance and the historical title, as against
the two bourgeois factions that only understood their own particular regime, of having asserted under the monarchy the
general regime of the bourgeois class, the nameless realm of the
republic, which they idealized and embellished with antique
arabesques, but in which, above all, they hailed the rule of their
coterie. If the party of the *National* grew confused in its own
mind when it descried the coalesced royalists at the head of the
republic founded by it, these royalists deceived themselves no
less concerning the fact of their united rule. They did not comprehend that if each of their factions, regarded by itself sepa-
rately, was royalist, the product of their chemical combination
had necessarily to be republican, that the white and the blue
monarchy had to neutralize each other in the tricolor republic.
Forced by antagonism to the revolutionary proletariat and
the transition classes thronging more and more round this as the
center, to summon their united strength and to conserve the
organization of this united strength, each faction of the party
of order, as against the desires for restoration and overweening
presumptions of the other, had to assert their joint rule, *i.e.*,
the republican form of bourgeois rule. Thus we find these
royalists in the beginning believing in an immediate restoration,
later preserving the republican form with foaming rage and
deadly invective against it on their lips, and finally confessing
that they can endure each other only in the republic and post-
poning the restoration indefinitely. The enjoyment of the united
rule itself strengthened each of the two factions, and made each
of them still more unable and unwilling to subordinate itself to
the other, *i.e.*, to restore the monarchy.

The party of order directly proclaimed in its election program the rule of the bourgeoisie, *i.e.*, the maintenance of the
life-conditions of its rule, property, the family, religion, order!
Naturally it represented its class rule and the conditions of its
class rule as the rule of civilization and as the necessary conditions of material production as well as of the social relations
arising from it. The party of order had enormous money resources at its command; it organized its branches throughout

France; it had all the ideologues of the old society in its pay; it had the influence of the existing governmental power at its disposal; it possessed an army of unpaid vassals in the whole mass of petty bourgeois and peasants, who, still far removed from the revolutionary movement, found in the high dignitaries of property the natural representatives of their petty property and its petty prejudices. This party, represented throughout the country by countless petty kings, could punish the rejection of their candidates as insurrection, dismiss the rebellious workers, the recalcitrant farm hands, servants, clerks, railway officials, penmen, all the functionaries civilly subordinate to it. Finally, here and there, it could maintain the delusion that the republican Constituent Assembly had obstructed the Bonaparte of December 10 in the manifestation of his wonder-working powers. We have not mentioned the Bonapartists in connection with the party of order. They were not a serious faction of the bourgeois class, but a collection of old, superstitious invalids and young, skeptical fortune-hunters. The party of order was victorious in the elections; it sent a large majority into the Legislative Assembly.

As against the coalesced counter-revolutionary bourgeois class, the sections of the petty bourgeoisie and peasant class already revolutionized had naturally to join up with the high dignitary of revolutionary interests, the revolutionary proletariat. We have seen how the democratic spokesmen of the petty bourgeoisie in Parliament, *i.e.*, the Mountain, were driven by parliamentary defeats to the socialist spokesmen of the proletariat, and how the actual petty bourgeoisie, outside of Parliament, were driven by the *concordats à l'amiable*, by the brutal enforcement of bourgeois interests and by bankruptcy to the actual proletarians. On January 27, Mountain and Socialists had celebrated their reconciliation, and at the great banquet of February 1849, they repeated their act of union. The social and the democratic, the party of the workers and that of the petty bourgeois, were united into the Social-Democratic Party, *i.e.*, the Red party.

The French republic, paralyzed for a moment by the agony

that followed the June days, had lived through a continuous series of feverish excitements since the raising of the state of siege, since October 14. First the struggle for the Presidency, then the struggle between the President and the Constituent Assembly; the struggle for the clubs; the trial in Bourges,[51] which, in contrast to the petty figures of the President, the coalesced royalists, the honest republicans, the democratic Mountain and the socialist doctrinaires of the proletariat, caused the proletariat's real revolutionaries to appear as antediluvian monsters, such as only a deluge could leave behind on the surface of society, or such as could only precede a social flood; the election agitation, the execution of the Bréa murderers; [52] the continual proceedings against the press; the violent interference of the government with the banquets by police action; the insolent royalist provocations; the exhibition of the portraits of Louis Blanc and Caussidière on the pillory; [53] the unbroken struggle between the constituted republic and the Constituent Assembly, which each moment drove the revolution back to its starting point, which each moment made the victors the vanquished and the vanquished the victors and, in a trice, changed the positions of the parties and the classes, their separations and connections; the rapid march of the European counter-revolution; the glorious Hungarian fight; the armed uprisings in Germany; the Roman expedition; the ignominious defeat of the French army before Rome—in this vortex of the movement, in this torment of historical unrest, in this dramatic ebb and flow of revolutionary passions, hopes, disappointments, the different classes of French society had to count their epochs of development in weeks where they had previously counted them in half centuries. A considerable section of the peasants and of the provinces was revolutionized. Not only were they disappointed in Napoleon, but the Red party offered them, instead of the name, the content, instead of illusory freedom from taxation, repayment of the milliard paid to the Legitimists, the regulation of mortgages and the suppression of usurers.

The army itself was infected with the revolutionary fever. In voting for Bonaparte it had voted for victory, and he gave it defeat. In him it had voted for the Little Corporal, behind whom the great revolutionary general was concealed, and he gave it once more the great generals, behind whom sheltered the pipe-clay corporal. There was no doubt that the Red party, *i.e.*, the united democratic party, was bound to celebrate, if not victory, still, great triumphs; that Paris, the army and a great part of the provinces would vote for it. Ledru-Rollin, the leader of the Mountain, was elected by five departments; no chief of the party of order bore off such a victory, no candidate belonging to the true proletarian party. This election reveals to us the secret of the democratic-socialist party.

If, on the one hand, the Mountain, the parliamentary champion of the democratic petty bourgeoisie, was forced to unite with the socialist doctrinaires of the proletariat—the proletariat, forced by the terrible material defeat of June to raise itself up again through intellectual victories and not yet enabled through the development of the remaining classes to seize the revolutionary dictatorship, had to throw itself into the arms of the doctrinaires of its emancipation, the founders of socialist sects —on the other hand, the revolutionary peasants, the army and the provinces ranged themselves behind the Mountain, which thus became the commander in the revolutionary army camp and through the understanding with the Socialists had eliminated every antagonism in the revolutionary party. In the last half of the life of the Constituent Assembly it represented the latter's revolutionary fervor and had buried in oblivion its sins during the Provisional Government, during the Executive Commission, during the June days. In the same measure as the party of the *National*, in accordance with its half-and-half nature, had allowed itself to be put down by the royalist ministry, the party of the Mountain, which had been brushed aside during the omnipotence of the *National*, rose and asserted itself as the parliamentary representative of the revolution. In fact, the party of the *National* had nothing to oppose to the other royalist factions but honors-hunting personalities and idealistic humbug. The party of the Mountain, on the contrary, represented a mass wavering between the bourgeoisie and the proletariat, whose material interests demanded democratic institutions. As against the Cavaignacs and the Marrasts, Ledru-Rollin and the Mountain therefore represented the truth of the revolution, and from the consciousness of this important situation they drew greater courage the more the expression of revolutionary energy limited itself to parliamentary attacks, bringing in bills of impeachment, threats, raised voices, thundering speeches, and extremes which were only pushed as far as phrases. The peasants were in about the same position as the petty bourgeoisie; they had more or less the same social demands to put forward. All the middle sections of society, so far as they were driven into the revolutionary movement, were therefore bound to find their revolutionary hero in Ledru-Rollin. Ledru-Rollin was the personage of the democratic petty bourgeoisie. As against the party of order, the half conservative, half revolutionary and wholly utopian reformers of this order had first to be pushed to the front.

The party of the *National*, the Friends of the Constitution *quand même*,* the *républicains purs et simples* † were completely defeated in the elections. A tiny minority of them was sent into the Legislative Chamber, their most notorious chiefs vanished from the stage, even Marrast, the editor *en chef* and the Orpheus of the honest republic.

On May 29 the Legislative Assembly met; on June 11, the collision of May 8 was renewed and, in the name of the Mountain, Ledru-Rollin brought in a bill of impeachment against the President and the ministry for violation of the constitution, and for the bombardment of Rome. On June 12, the Legislative Assembly rejected the bill of impeachment as the Constituent Assembly had rejected it on May 11, but the proletariat this time drove the Mountain onto the streets, not to a street fight, however, only to a street procession. It is enough to say that the Mountain was at the head of this movement to know that the movement was defeated, and that June 1849 was a caricature, as laughable as it was futile, of June 1848. The great retreat

* All the same.
† Republicans pure and simple.

of June 13 was only eclipsed by the still greater battle-report of Changarnier, the great man that the party of order improvised. Every social epoch needs its great men, and when it does not find them, it invents them, as Helvetius says.

On December 20 only one-half of the constituted bourgeois republic was still in existence, the President; on May 29 it was completed by the other half, the Legislative Assembly. In June, 1848, the constituent bourgeois republic, by an unspeakable blow against the proletariat, in June, 1849, the constituted bourgeois republic, by an unutterable comedy with the petty bourgeoisie, had inscribed itself in the birth-register of history. June, 1849, was the nemesis of June, 1848. In June, 1849, it was not the workers that were vanquished; it was the petty bourgeois, standing between them and the revolution that were felled; June 1849, was not a bloody tragedy between wage-labor and capital, but a prison-filling and lamentable play of debtors and creditors. The party of order had won, it was all-powerful; it had now to show what it was.

III

FROM JUNE 13, 1849, TO MARCH 10, 1850

(*From Number III*)

On December 20, the Janus head of the constitutional republic had still shown only one face, the executive face with the indistinct, plain features of L. Bonaparte; on May 29, 1849, it showed its second face, the legislative, pitted with the scars that the orgies of the restoration and the July monarchy had left behind. With the Legislative National Assembly the constitutional republic was completed, *i.e.*, the republican form of state, in which the rule of the bourgeois class is constituted, therefore the common rule of the two great royalist factions that form the French bourgeoisie, of the coalesced Legitimists and Orleanists, of the party of order. While the French republic thus became the property of the coalition of the royalist parties, at the same time the European coalition of the counter-revolutionary powers began a general crusade against the last places of refuge of the March revolutions. Russia invaded Hungary; Prussia marched against the army defending the imperial constitution, and Oudinot bombarded Rome. The European crisis was evidently approaching a decisive turning point; the eyes of all Europe were turned on Paris, and the eyes of all Paris on the Legislative Assembly.

On June 11 Ledru-Rollin mounted its tribune. He made no speech; he formulated a requisitory * against the ministers, naked, unadorned, factual, concentrated, forceful.

The attack on Rome is an attack on the constitution; the attack on the Roman republic is an attack on the French re-

---

* In French law, the demand of the public prosecutor for punishment of the accused.

public. Article V of the constitution reads: "The French republic never employs its military forces against the liberty of any people whatsoever"—and the President employs the French army against Roman liberty. Article IV of the constitution forbids the executive power to declare any war whatsoever without the assent of the National Assembly. The Constituent Assembly's resolution of May 8 expressly commands the ministers to make the Rome expedition conform with the utmost speed to its original mission; it therefore just as expressly prohibits war on Rome—and Oudinot bombards Rome. Thus Ledru-Rollin called the constitution itself as a witness for the prosecution against Bonaparte and his ministers. At the royalist majority of the National Assembly, he, the tribune of the constitution, hurled the threatening declaration: "The republicans will know how to command respect for the constitution by every means, be it even by the force of arms!" "By the force of arms!" repeated the hundredfold echo of the Mountain. The majority answered with a terrible tumult; the President of the National Assembly called Ledru-Rollin to order; Ledru-Rollin repeated the challenging declaration, and finally laid on the President's table a motion for the impeachment of Bonaparte and his ministers. By 361 votes to 203, the National Assembly resolved to pass on from the bombardment of Rome to the simple order of the day.

Did Ledru-Rollin believe that he could beat the National Assembly by means of the constitution, and the President by means of the National Assembly?

To be sure, the constitution forbade any attack on the liberty of foreign peoples, but what the French army attacked in Rome, was, according to the ministry, not "liberty" but the "despotism of anarchy." Had the Mountain still not comprehended, all experiences in the Constituent Assembly notwithstanding, that the interpretation of the constitution did not belong to those who had made it, but only to those who had accepted it? That the letter must be construed in its living meaning and that the bourgeois meaning was its only living meaning? That Bonaparte and the royalist majority of the National Assembly were the authentic interpreters of the constitution, as the priest is the authentic interpreter of the bible, and the judge the authentic interpreter of the law? Should the National Assembly, fresh from the midst of the general elections, feel itself bound by the testamentary provisions of the dead Constituent Assembly, whose living will an Odilon Barrot had broken? When Ledru-Rollin cited the Constituent Assembly's resolution on May 8, had he forgotten that the same Constituent Assembly on May 11 had rejected his motion for the impeachment of Bonaparte and the ministers; that it had acquitted the President and the ministers; that it had thus sanctioned the attack on Rome as "constitutional"; that he only lodged an appeal against a judgment already delivered; that he finally appealed from the republican Constituent Assembly to the royalist Legislative? The constitution itself calls the insurrection to its aid, by summoning, in a special article, every citizen to protect it. Ledru-Rollin based himself on this article. But, at the same time, are not the public powers organized for the defense of the constitution, and does not the violation of the constitution first begin from the moment when one of the public constitutional powers rebels against the other? And the President of the republic, the ministers of the republic and the National Assembly of the republic were in the most harmonious agreement.

What the Mountain attempted on June 11 was "an insurrection within the limits of pure reason," *i.e.*, a purely parliamentary insurrection. The majority of the Assembly, intimidated by the prospect of an armed rising of the popular masses, was, in the persons of Bonaparte and the ministers, to destroy its own power and the significance of its own election. Had not the Constituent Assembly similarly attempted to annul the election of Bonaparte, when it insisted so obstinately on the dismissal of the Barrot-Falloux ministry?

Neither were there lacking from the time of the Convention models for parliamentary insurrections, which had suddenly transformed completely the relation between the majority and the minority—and should the young Mountain not succeed where the old had succeeded?—nor did the relations at the moment seem unfavorable for such an undertaking. The popular unrest had in Paris reached a critically high point; the army, according to its voting at the election, did not seem inclined towards the government; the legislative majority itself was still too young to have consolidated itself and, in addition, it consisted of old gentlemen. If the Mountain were successful in a parliamentary insurrection, then the helm of state fell directly into its hands. The democratic petty bourgeoisie, for its part, wished, as always, for nothing more fervently than to see the battle fought out in the clouds over its head between the departed spirits of parliament. Finally both of them, the democratic petty bourgeoisie and its representatives, the Mountain, through a parliamentary insurrection achieved their great purpose, that of breaking the power of the bourgeoisie, without unleashing the proletariat, or letting it appear otherwise than in perspective; the proletariat would have been used without becoming dangerous.

After the vote of the National Assembly on June 11, a conference took place between some members of the Mountain and delegates of the workers' secret societies. The latter pressed for striking the first blow the same evening. The Mountain decisively rejected this plan. On no account did it want to let the leadership slip out of its hands; its allies were as suspect to it as its antagonists, and rightly so. The memory of June 1848 surged through the ranks of the Paris proletariat more vigorously than ever. Nevertheless it was chained to the alliance with the Mountain. The latter represented the largest part of the departments; it exaggerated its influence in the army; it had at its disposal the democratic section of the National Guard; it had the moral power of the shop behind it. To begin the revolution at this moment against the will of the Mountain, meant for the proletariat, decimated moreover by cholera and driven out of Paris in considerable numbers by unemployment, to repeat the June days of 1848 uselessly, without the situation which had forced this desperate struggle. The proletarian delegates did the only rational thing. They bound the Mountain to compromise itself, *i.e.*, to come out beyond the confines of the parliamentary struggle in the event of its bill of impeachment being rejected. During the whole of June 13, the proletariat maintained this same skeptically watchful attitude, and awaited a seriously engaged irrevocable *mêlée* between the democratic National Guard and the army, in order then to plunge into the fight and push the revolution forward beyond the petty-bourgeois aim set for it. In the event of victory the proletarian commune was already formed which would take its place beside the official government. The Parisian workers had learned in the bloody school of June, 1848.

On June 12 the Minister Lacrosse himself brought forward in the Legislative Assembly the motion to proceed at once to the discussion of the bill of impeachment. During the night the government made every provision for defense and attack; the majority of the National Assembly was determined to drive out the rebellious minority into the streets; the minority itself could no longer retreat; the die was cast; the bill of impeachment was rejected by 377 votes to 8. The Mountain, which had abstained from voting, rushed muttering into the propaganda halls of the "pacific democracy," into the newspaper offices of the *Démocratie pacifique*.*

Its withdrawal from the House of Parliament broke its strength as withdrawal from the earth broke the strength of Antaeus, her giant son. Samsons in the precincts of the Legislative Assembly, they were only Philistines in the precincts of the "pacific democracy." A long, noisy, rambling debate began. The Mountain was determined to compel respect for the constitution by every means, "only not by force of arms." In this decision it was supported by a manifesto and by a deputation of the "Friends of the Constitution." "Friends of the Constitution," was what the wreckage of the coterie of the *National*, of the bourgeois-republican party called itself. While six of its remaining parliamentary representatives had voted against, the others in a body voting for the rejection of the bill of impeachment; while Cavaignac placed his saber at the disposal of the party of order, the larger, extra-parliamentary part of the coterie

* The organ of the Fourierists, edited by Considérant.

greedily seized the opportunity to emerge from its position of a political pariah, and to press into the ranks of the democratic party. Did they not appear as the natural shield bearers of this party, which hid itself behind their shield, behind their principles, behind the constitution?

Till break of day the "Mountain" was in labor. It gave birth to "a proclamation to the people," which, on the morning of June 13, occupied a more or less shamefaced place in two socialist journals. It declared the President, the ministers, the majority of the Legislative Assembly "outside the constitution" (*hors la constitution*) and summoned the National Guard, the army and finally the people "to arise." "Long live the constitution!" was the slogan that it gave out, a slogan that signified nothing other than "Down with the revolution!"

In conformity with the constitutional proclamation of the Mountain, there was a so-called peaceful demonstration of the petty bourgeois on June 13, *i.e.*, a street procession from the *Château d'Eau* through the boulevards, 30,000 strong, mainly National Guards, unarmed and with an admixture of members of the workers' secret sections, moving along with the cry: "Long live the constitution," which was uttered mechanically, ice-coldly and with a bad conscience by the members of the procession itself, and thrown back ironically by the echo of the people that surged along the side-walks, instead of swelling up like thunder. From the many voiced song the chest notes were missing. And when the procession swung by the meeting hall of the "Friends of the Constitution" and a hired herald of the constitution appeared on the house-top, violently cleaving the air with his *claquer* * hat and from tremendous lungs letting the catch-cry "Long live the constitution" fall like hail on the heads of the pilgrims, they seemed themselves overcome for a moment by the comedy of the situation. It is well known how the procession, having arrived at the entrance of the Rue de la Paix, was received in the boulevards by the dragoons and riflemen of Changarnier in an altogether unparliamentary way, how in a trice it scattered in all directions and how it threw behind it a

* *Claquer:* one who is paid to clap in the theater.

few shouts of "To arms" only in order that the parliamentary call to arms of June 11 might be fulfilled.

The majority of the Mountain assembled in the Rue du Hazard dispersed, when this violent disruption of the peaceful procession, the muffled rumors of murder of unarmed citizens on the boulevards and the growing tumult in the streets seemed to herald the approach of a rising. Ledru-Rollin at the head of a small band of deputies saved the honor of the Mountain. Under the protection of the Paris Artillery which had assembled in the Palais National, they betook themselves to the *Conservatoire des Arts et Métiers,* where the fifth and sixth legions of the National Guard were to arrive. But the *montagnards* * waited in vain for the fifth and sixth legions; these discreet National Guards left their representatives in the lurch; the Paris Artillery itself prevented the people from throwing up barricades; a chaotic disorder made any decision impossible; the troops of the line advanced with fixed bayonets; some of the representatives were taken prisoner; while others escaped. Thus ended June 13.

If June 23, 1848, was the insurrection of the revolutionary proletariat, June 13, 1849, was the insurrection of the democratic petty bourgeois, each of these two insurrections being the classically pure expression of the class which had made it.

Only in Lyons did it come to an obstinate, bloody conflict. Here, where the industrial bourgeoisie and the industrial proletariat stand directly opposed to one another, where the workers' movement is not, as in Paris, included in and determined by the general movement, June 13, in its reactions, lost its original character. Where it broke out elsewhere in the provinces it did not kindle fire—a cold lightning-flash.

June 13 closes the first period of the Constitutional Republic, which had attained its normal span with the meeting of the Legislative Assembly in May. The whole period of this prologue is filled with noisy struggle between the party of order and the Mountain, between the bourgeoisie and the petty bourgeoisie, which strove in vain against the consolidation of the bourgeois republic, for which it had itself continuously conspired in the

* Members of the Mountain.

Provisional Government and in the Executive Commission, and for which, during the June days, it had fought fanatically against the proletariat. The 13th of June breaks its resistance and makes the legislative dictatorship of the united royalists a *fait accompli.** From this moment the National Assembly is only a committee of public safety of the party of order.

Paris had put the President, the ministers and the majority of the National Assembly in a "state of impeachment"; they put Paris in a "state of siege." The Mountain had declared the majority of the Legislative Assembly "outside the constitution"; for violation of the constitution the majority handed over the Mountain to the *haute cour* † and proscribed everything in it that still had vital force. It was decimated to a rump without head or heart. The minority had gone as far as to attempt a parliamentary insurrection; the majority elevated its parliamentary despotism to law. It decreed new standing orders, which annihilate the freedom of the tribune and authorize the president of the National Assembly to punish the representatives for infringement of the standing orders with censorship, with fines, with withdrawal of the indemnity moneys, with temporary expulsion, with incarceration. It hung over the rump of the Mountain the whip instead of the sword. The remainder of the deputies of the Mountain had owed it to their honor to make a mass exit. By such an act the dissolution of the party of order would have been hastened. It must have broken up into its original component parts from the moment when not even the appearance of an opposition held it together any longer.

Simultaneously with their parliamentary power, the democratic petty bourgeois were robbed of their armed power through the dissolution of the Paris Artillery and the 8th, 9th and 12th legions of the National Guard. On the other hand, the legion of high finance, which had raided the print shops of Boulé and Roux on June 13, destroyed the presses, played havoc with the offices of the republican journals and arbitrarily arrested editors, compositors, printers, dispatch clerks and errand boys, received

* Accomplished fact.
† High court.

the most stirring encouragement from the tribune of the National Assembly. All over France the dissolution of the National Guards suspected of republicanism was repeated.

A new press law, a new law of association, a new law on the state of siege, the prisons of Paris overflowing, the political fugitives driven out, all the journals that go beyond the limits of the *National* suspended, Lyons and the five departments surrounding it surrendered to the brutal chicanery of military despotism, the *parquets* * ubiquitous and the army of officials so often purged, purged once more—these were the inevitable, the constantly recurring commonplaces of victorious reaction, only worth mentioning after the massacres and the deportations of June, because this time they were directed not only against Paris, but also against the departments, not only against the proletariat, but, above all, against the middle classes.

The repressive laws, by which the declaration of a state of siege was left to the discretion of the government, the press still more firmly muzzled and the right of association annihilated, absorbed the whole of the legislative activity of the National Assembly, during the months of June, July and August.

Nevertheless, this epoch is characterized not by the exploitation of victory in fact, but in principle; not by the resolutions of the National Assembly, but by the grounds advanced for these resolutions; not by the thing, but by the phrase; not by the phrase but by the accent and the gesture which enliven the phrase. The unreserved, unashamed expression of royalist sentiments, the contemptuously aristocratic insults to the republic, the coquettishly frivolous babbling of the restoration aims, in a word, the boastful violation of republican decorum, give its peculiar tone and color to this period. Long live the constitution! was the battle-cry of the vanquished of June 13. The victors were therefore absolved from the hypocrisy of constitutional, *i.e.*, republican, speech. The counter-revolution conquered in Hungary, Italy and Germany, and it believed that the restoration was already at the gates of France. Among the masters of ceremonies of the factions of order, there ensued a

* *Parquet:* office of the public prosecutor.

real competition to document their royalism in the *Moniteur,* and to confess, repent and beg pardon before God and man for liberal sins perchance committed by them under the republic. No day passed without the February Revolution being declared a public misfortune from the tribune of the National Assembly, without some Legitimist provincial cabbage-Junker solemnly stating that he had never recognized the republic, without one of the cowardly deserters and traitors of the July monarchy relating the belated deeds of heroism in the performance of which only the philanthropy of Louis Philippe or other mis-understandings hindered him. What was admirable in the February days was not the magnanimity of the victorious people, but the self-sacrifice and moderation of the royalists, who had allowed it to be victorious. One representative of the people proposed to divert part of the money destined for the relief of those wounded in February to the Municipal Guards, who alone in those days had deserved well of the fatherland. Another wanted to have an equestrian statue decreed to the Duke of Orleans in the *Place de Carrousel.* Thiers called the constitution a dirty piece of paper. There appeared in succession on the tribune Orleanists, to repent of their conspiracy against the legitimate monarchy; Legitimists, who reproached themselves with having hastened the overthrow of monarchy in general by resisting the illegitimate monarchy; Thiers, who repented of having intrigued against Molé; Molé, who repented of having intrigued against Guizot; Barrot, who repented of having intrigued against all three. The cry "Long live the Social-Democratic republic!" was declared unconstitutional: the cry "Long live the republic!" was prosecuted as social-democratic. On the anniversary of the Battle of Waterloo, a deputy declared: "I fear an invasion of the Prussians less than the entry of the revolutionary refugees into France." To the complaints about the terrorism which was organized in Lyons and in the neighboring departments, Baraguay d'Hilliers answered: "I prefer the White terror to the Red terror." (*J'aime mieux la terreur blanche que la terreur rouge.*) And the Assembly applauded frantically every time that an epigram against the republic, against the revolution, against the constitution, for the monarchy or for the Holy Alliance fell from the lips of its orators. Every infringement of the minutest republican formalities, for example, addressing the representatives as *citoyens*, filled the knights of order with enthusiasm.

The by-election in Paris on July 8, held under the influence of the state of siege and of the abstention of a great part of the proletariat from the ballot box, the taking of Rome by the French army, the entry of the red eminences * into Rome and, in their train, the inquisition and monkish terrorism, added fresh victories to the victory of June and increased the intoxication of the party of order.

Finally, in the middle of August, half with the intention of attending the Department Councils just assembled, half through exhaustion from the tendencious orgy of many months, the royalists decreed the prorogation of the National Assembly for two months. With transparent irony, they left behind a commission of twenty-five representatives, the cream of the Legitimists and the Orleanists, a Molé and a Changarnier, as proxies for the National Assembly and as guardians of the republic. The irony was more profound than they suspected. They, condemned by history to help to overthrow the monarchy they loved, were destined by her to conserve the republic they hated.

The second period in the life of the constitutional republic, its period of royalist boorishness, closes with the proroguing of the Legislative Assembly.

The state of siege in Paris was again raised, the activities of the press had again begun. During the suspension of the Social Democratic papers, during the period of repressive legislation and royalist blusters, the *Siècle*, the old literary representative of the monarchist-constitutional petty bourgeois, republicanized itself; the *Presse*, the old literary expression of the bourgeois reformers, democratized itself; while the *National*, the old classic organ of the republican bourgeois, socialized itself.

The secret societies grew in extent and intensity in the measure that the public clubs became impossible. The industrial associa-

* Cardinals.

tions of workers, tolerated as purely trade companies, while of no account economically, became politically so many means of cementing the proletariat. June 13 had struck off the official heads of the different semi-revolutionary parties; the masses that remained won their own head. The knights of order had intimidated the Red republic by prophecies of terror; the base excesses, the hyperborean atrocities of the victorious counter-revolution in Hungary, in Baden and in Rome washed the "Red republic" white. And the discontented intermediate classes of French society began to prefer the promises of the Red republic with its problematic terrors to the terrors of the red monarchy with its actual hopelessness. No Socialist in France did more actual revolutionary propaganda than Haynau.[54] *A chaque capacité selon ses oeuvres!* *

In the meantime Louis Bonaparte exploited the recess of the National Assembly by making princely tours of the provinces, the most hot-blooded Legitimists made pilgrimages to Ems, to the grandchild of the saintly Ludwig, and the mass of the popular representatives on the side of order intrigued in the department councils, which had just met. It was necessary to make them pronounce what the majority of the National Assembly did not yet dare to pronounce, an urgent motion for immediate revision of the constitution. According to the constitution, the constitution could only be revised in 1852 by a National Assembly called together expressly for this purpose. If, however, the majority of the department councils expressed themselves in this sense, was not the National Assembly bound to sacrifice the virginity of the constitution to the voice of France? The National Assembly entertained the same hopes in regard to these provincial assemblies as the nuns in Voltaire's *Henriade* entertained in regard to the pandours.† But, some exceptions apart, the Potiphars of the National Assembly had to deal with just so many Josephs of the provinces. The vast majority did not want to understand the importunate insinuation. The revi-

* To each capacity according to its works.
† Hungarian foot-soldiers in the Austrian service, so called from Pandur, a village in Hungary where they were first raised.

sion of the constitution was frustrated by the very instruments by which it was to have been called into being, by the votes of the department councils. The voice of France, and indeed of bourgeois France, had spoken and had spoken against revision.

At the beginning of October the Legislative Assembly met once more—*tantum mutatus ab illo.**—Its lineaments were completely changed. The unexpected rejection of revision on the part of the department councils had put it back within the limits of the constitution and indicated the limits of its term of life. The Orleanists had become mistrustful because of the pilgrimages of the Legitimists to Ems; the Legitimists had grown suspicious on account of the negotiations of the Orleanists with London; [55] the journals of the two factions had fanned the fire and weighed the reciprocal claims of their pretenders. Orleanists and Legitimists grumbled in unison concerning the machinations of the Bonapartists, which showed themselves in the princely tours, in the more or less obvious emancipatory attempts of the President, in the presumptuous language of the Bonapartist newspaper; Louis Bonaparte grumbled concerning the National Assembly, which found only the Legitimist-Orleanist conspiracy legitimate, concerning the ministry, which betrayed him continually to this National Assembly. Finally, the ministry was itself divided on the Roman policy and on the income tax proposed by the Minister Passy, and decried as socialistic by the conservatives.

One of the first bills of the Barrot ministry in the re-assembled Legislative was a demand for a credit of 300,000 francs for the payment of a widow's pension to the Duchess of Orleans. The National Assembly granted it and added to the list of debts of the French nation a sum of seven million francs. Thus while Louis Philippe continued to play with success the role of the *pauvre honteux*, of the ashamed beggar, the ministry neither dared to move an increase of salary for Bonaparte nor did the Assembly appear inclined to grant it. And Louis Bonaparte, as ever, vacillated in the dilemma: *Aut Cæsar aut Clichy!* †

* How greatly changed from the former.
† Either Cæsar or Clichy!

The minister's second demand for a credit, one of nine million francs for the costs of the Rome expedition, increased the tension between Bonaparte, on the one hand, and the ministers and the National Assembly, on the other. Louis Bonaparte had inserted a letter to his orderly officer Edgar Ney in the *Moniteur*, in which he bound the papist government to constitutional guarantees. The Pope, for his part, had published an address, *motu proprio*,* in which he rejected any limitation of his restored rule. Bonaparte's letter, with considered indiscretion, raised the curtain of his cabinet, in order to expose himself to the eyes of the gallery as a benevolent genius who was, however, misunderstood and shackled in his own house. It was not the first time that he had coquetted with the "timid flights of a free soul." Thiers, the reporter of the commission, completely ignored Bonaparte's flight and contented himself with translating the papist allocution into French. It was not the ministry, but Victor Hugo that sought to save the President through an order of the day in which the National Assembly was to express its agreement with Napoleon's letter. *Allons donc! Allons donc!* † With this disrespectful, frivolous interjection the majority buried Hugo's motion. The policy of the President? The letter of the President? The President himself? *Allons donc! Allons donc!* Who the devil takes Monsieur Bonaparte *au sérieux?* ‡ Do you believe, Monsieur Victor Hugo, that we believe you, that you believe in the President? *Allons donc! Allons donc!*

Finally, the breach between Bonaparte and the National Assembly was hastened by the discussion on the recall of the Orleanists and the Bourbons. In the default of the ministry, the cousin of the President, the son of the ex-king of Westphalia, had put forward this motion, which had no other purpose than to push the Legitimist and the Orleanist pretenders down to the same level, or rather a lower level than the Bonapartist pretender, who at least stood in fact at the head of the state.

---

* Of his own free will.
† Get along with you!
‡ Seriously.

Napoleon Bonaparte was disrespectful enough to make the recall of the expelled royal families and the amnesty of the June insurgents parts of one and the same motion. The indignation of the majority compelled him immediately to apologize for this sacrilegious joining of the holy and the impious, of the royal races and the proletarian brood, of the fixed stars of society and of its swamp lights, and to assign to each of the two motions the position proper to it. The majority energetically rejected the recall of the royal family, and Berryer, the Demosthenes of the Legitimists, left no doubt about the meaning of the vote. The civic degradation of the pretenders, that is what is intended! It is desired to rob them of their halo, of the last majesty that is left to them, the majesty of exile! What, cried Berryer, would be thought of him among the pretenders who, forgetting his august origin, came here to live as a simple private individual? It could not have been more clearly intimated to Louis Bonaparte that he had not gained the day by his presence, that if the royalists in coalition needed him here in France as a neutral person in the President's chair, the serious pretenders to the throne had to be kept out of profane sight by the fog of exile.

On November 1, Louis Bonaparte answered the Legislative Assembly with a message which in pretty sharp words announced the dismissal of the Barrot ministry and the formation of a new ministry. The Barrot-Falloux ministry was the ministry of the royalist coalition, the d'Hautpoul ministry was the ministry of Bonaparte, the organ of the President as against the Legislative Assembly, the ministry of the clerks.

Bonaparte was no longer the merely neutral man of December 10, 1848. Possession of the executive power had grouped a number of interests around him, the struggle with anarchy forced the party of order even to increase his influence, and if he was no longer popular, the party of order was unpopular. Could he not hope to compel the Orleanists and the Legitimists, through their rivalry as well as through the necessity of some sort of monarchist restoration, to recognize the neutral President?

From November 1, 1849, dates the third period in the life of the constitutional republic, a period which closes with March 10, 1850. Not only does the regular play, so much admired by Guizot, of the constitutional institutions now begin, but the quarrel between executive and legislative power. As against the hankerings for restoration on the part of the united Orleanists and Legitimists, Bonaparte represents the title of his actual power, the republic; as against the hankerings for restoration on the part of Bonaparte, the party of order represents the title of its common rule, the republic; as against the Orleanists, the Legitimists and as against the Legitimists, the Orleanists represent the *status quo*,* the republic. All these factions of the party of order, each of which has its own king and its own restoration *in petto*,† mutually assert, as against their rivals' desires for usurpation and elevation, the common rule of the bourgeoisie, the form in which the particular claims remain neutralized and reserved—the republic.

Just as Kant makes the republic, as the only rational form of state, a postulate of practical reason whose realization is never attained, but whose attainment must always be striven for and mentally adhered to as the goal, so these royalists make the monarchy.

Thus the constitutional republic had gone forth from the hands of the bourgeois republicans as a hollow ideological formula, to a form full of content and life in the hands of the royalists, in coalition. And Thiers spoke more truly than he suspected, when he said: "We, the royalists, are the true pillars of the constitutional republic."

The overthrow of the ministry of the coalition, and the appearance of the ministry of the clerks has a second significance. Its finance minister was Fould. Fould as finance minister signifies the official surrender of French national wealth to the Bourse, the management of the state's property by the Bourse and in the interest of the Bourse. With the nomination of Fould, the finance aristocracy announced its restoration in the *Moniteur*.

* Unchanged position.
† In reserve.

This restoration necessarily supplemented the other restorations, which form just so many links in the chain of the constitutional republic.

Louis Philippe had never dared to make a real *loup-cervier*, (Bourse wolf) finance minister. Just as his monarchy was the ideal name for the rule of the high bourgeoisie, in his ministries the privileged interests had to bear ideologically neutral names. The bourgeois republic everywhere pushed into the forefront what the different monarchies, Legitimist as well as Orleanist, kept concealed in the background. It made earthly what they had made heavenly. In place of the names of the saints, it put the bourgeois proper names of the ruling class interests.

Our whole exposition has shown how the republic, from the first day of its existence, did not overthrow the finance aristocracy, but consolidated it. But the concessions that were made to it were a fate to which submission was made without the desire to bring it about. With Fould, the initiative in the government returned to the finance aristocracy.

The question will be asked how the bourgeoisie in coalition could bear and suffer the rule of finance, which under Louis Philippe depended on the exclusion or subordination of the remaining bourgeois factions.

The answer is simple.

First of all, the finance aristocracy itself forms a weighty, authoritative part of the royalist coalition, whose common governmental power is the republic. Are not the spokesmen and leading lights among the Orleanists the old confederates and accomplices of the finance aristocracy? Is it not itself the golden phalanx of Orleanism? As far as the Legitimists are concerned, in practice they had already participated in all the orgies of the Bourse, mine and railway speculations under Louis Philippe. In general, the combination of large landed property with high finance is a normal factor. Proof: England; proof: even Austria.

In a country like France, where the volume of national production stands at a disproportionately lower level than the amount of the national debt, where the state revenue forms the most important subject of speculation and the Bourse the chief market for the investment of capital that wants to turn itself to account in an unproductive way—in such a country a countless number of people of all bourgeois or semi-bourgeois classes must participate in the state debt, in the Bourse gamblings, in finance. Do not all these subaltern participants find their natural mainstays and commanders in the faction which represents this interest in its vastest outlines, which represents it as a whole?

By what is the reversion of the state property to high finance conditioned? By the constantly growing indebtedness of the state. And the indebtedness of the state? By the constant excess of its expenditure over its income, a disproportion which is simultaneously the cause and effect of the system of state loans.

In order to escape from this indebtedness, the state must either restrict its expenditure, *i.e.*, simplify and curtail the government organism, govern as little as possible, employ as small a personnel as possible, enter as little into relations with bourgeois society as possible. This path was impossible for the party of order, whose means of repression, whose official interference for reasons of state and whose universal presence through organs of state were bound to increase in the same measure as its rule and the life-conditions of its class were threatened from more numerous sides. The *gendarmerie* could not be reduced in the same measure as attacks on persons and property increase.

Or the state must seek to elude the debts and produce an immediate but transitory balance in its budget, by putting extraordinary taxes on the shoulders of the wealthiest classes. In order to withdraw the national wealth from exploitation by the Bourse, was the party of order to sacrifice its own wealth on the altar of the fatherland? *Pas si bête!* *

Therefore, without a complete revolution in the French state, no revolution in the French state's budget. Along with this state budget necessarily goes state indebtedness, and with state indebtedness necessarily goes the rule of the trade in state debts, of the state creditors, the bankers, the money dealers and the wolves of the Bourse. Only a fraction of the party of order was directly concerned in the overthrow of the finance aristoc-

* Not so stupid.

racy—the manufacturers. We are not speaking of the middle, of the smaller industrials; we are speaking of the rulers of the factory interest, who had formed the broad basis of the dynastic opposition under Louis Philippe. Their interest is indubitably reduction of the costs of production, therefore reduction of the taxes, which enter into production, therefore reduction of the state debts, the interest on which enters into the taxes, therefore the overthrow of the finance aristocracy.

In England—and the largest French manufacturers are petty bourgeois as against their English rivals—we really find the manufacturers, a Cobden, a Bright, at the head of the crusade against the bank and the stock exchange aristocracy. Why not in France? In England industry rules; in France, agriculture. In England industry requires free trade; in France, protection, national monopoly besides other monopolies. French industry does not dominate French production; the French industrialists, therefore, do not dominate the French bourgeoisie. In order to put through their interest against the remaining fractions of the bourgeoisie, they cannot, like the English, take the lead of the movement and simultaneously push their class interest to the fore; they must follow in the train of the revolution, and serve interests which are opposed to the collective interests of their class. In February they had misunderstood their position; February sharpened their wits. And who is more directly threatened by the workers than the employer, the industrial capitalist? The manufacturer, therefore, of necessity became in France the most fanatical member of the party of order. The reduction of his profit by finance, what is that compared with the abolition of profit by the proletariat?

In France, the petty bourgeois does what normally the industrial bourgeois would have to do; the worker does what normally would be the task of the petty bourgeois, and the task of the worker, who solves that? No one. It is not solved in France; it is proclaimed in France. It is not solved anywhere within the national walls; the class war within French society turns into a world war, in which the nations confront one another. The solution begins only at the moment when, through the world war, the proletariat is pushed to the head of the people that dominates the world market, to the head of England. The revolution, which finds here, not its end, but its organizational beginning, is no short-lived revolution. The present generation is like the Jews, whom Moses led through the wilderness. It has not only a new world to conquer, it must go under, in order to make room for the men who are fit for a new world.

Let us return to Fould.

On November 14, 1849, Fould mounted the tribune of the National Assembly and expounded his system of finance: *Apologia* for the old system of taxes! Retention of the wine tax! Repeal of Passy's income tax!

Passy, too, was no revolutionary; he was an old minister of Louis Philippe's. He belonged to the puritans of the Dufaure brand and to the most intimate *confidants of Teste,** the scape-goat of the July monarchy. Passy, too, had praised the old tax system and recommended the retention of the wine tax; but he had, at the same time, torn the veil from the state deficit. He had declared the necessity for a new tax, the income tax, if it were desired to avoid the bankruptcy of the state. Fould, who recommended state bankruptcy to Ledru-Rollin, recommended the state deficit to the Legislative Assembly. He promised economies, the secret of which later revealed itself in that, for example, the expenditure diminished by sixty millions, while the floating debt increased by two hundred millions—conjuring tricks in the grouping of figures, in the drawing up of accounts rendered, which all finally resulted in new loans.

Alongside the other jealous bourgeois factions, the finance aristocracy under Fould naturally did not act in so shamelessly corrupt a manner as under Louis Philippe. But the system remained the same, constant increase in the debts and masking

---

*On June 18, 1849, before the Chamber of Peers in Paris, the trial of Parmentier and General Cubières began for bribery of officials with a view to obtaining a salt works concession and of the then Minister for Public Works, Teste, for accepting such money bribes. The latter, during the trial, attempted to commit suicide. All were sentenced to pay heavy fines; Teste, in addition, to serve three years' imprisonment. [Note by Frederick Engels.]

of the deficit. And, in time, the old Bourse swindling came out more openly. Proof: the law concerning the Avignon railway; the mysterious fluctuations in government stocks, for a brief space the topic of the hour throughout Paris; finally, the ill-starred speculations of Fould and Bonaparte on the elections of March 10.

With the official restoration of the finance aristocracy, the French people had soon again to stand before a February 24.

The Constituent Assembly, in an attack of misanthropy against its heir, had abolished the wine tax for the year of the Lord, 1850. With the abolition of old taxes, now debts could not be paid. *Creton,* a cretin of the party of order, before the proroguing of the Legislative Assembly, already moved the retention of the wine tax. Fould took up this motion in the name of the Bonapartist ministry and, on December 20, 1849, the anniversary of the proclamation of Bonaparte, the National Assembly decreed the restoration of the wine tax.

The sponsor of this restoration was not a financier; it was the Jesuit chief, *Montalembert.* His argument was strikingly simple: Taxation is the maternal breast on which the government is suckled. The government is the instrument of repression; it is the organ of authority; it is the army; it is the police; it is the officials, the judges, the ministers; it is the priests. The attack on taxation is the attack of the anarchists on the sentinels of order, who safeguard the material and spiritual production of bourgeois society from the inroads of the proletarian vandals. Taxation is the fifth god, side by side with property, the family, order and religion. And the wine tax is incontestably taxation and, moreover, not vulgar, but traditional, monarchically disposed, respectable taxation. *Vive l'impôt des boissons!* * Three cheers and one cheer more! †

The French peasant, when he paints the devil on the wall, paints him in the guise of the tax collector. From the moment when Montalembert elevated taxation to a god, the peasant became godless, atheist, and threw himself into the arms of the

* Long live the tax on drinks.
† In English in the original text.

devil, socialism. The religion of order had lost him; the Jesuits had lost him; Bonaparte had lost him. December 20, 1849, had irrevocably compromised December 20, 1848. The "nephew of his uncle" was not the first of his family whom the wine tax defeated, this tax which, in the expression of Montalembert, heralds the revolutionary storm. The real, the great Napoleon declared at St. Helena that the re-introduction of the wine tax had contributed more to his downfall than all else, since it had alienated from him the peasants of Southern France. Already the favorite object of the people's hate under Louis XIV (see the writings of Boisguillebert and Vauban), abolished by the first revolution, it was re-introduced by Napoleon in a modified form in 1808. When the restoration entered France, there trotted before it not only the Cossacks, but also the promises to abolish the wine tax. The *gentilhommerie* * naturally did not need to keep its word to the *gens taillable à merci et miséricorde.*† The year 1830 promised the abolition of the wine tax. It was not its way to do what it said or say what it did. 1848 promised the abolition of the wine tax as it promised everything. Finally, the Constituent Assembly, which promised nothing, made, as mentioned, a testamentary provision whereby the wine tax was to disappear on January 1, 1850. And just ten days before January 1, 1850, the Legislative Assembly introduced it once more, so that the French people perpetually pursued it and when it had thrown it out the door, saw it come in again through the window.

The popular hatred of the wine tax is explained by the fact that it unites in itself all the hatefulness of the French system of taxation. The mode of its collection is hateful, the mode of its distribution aristocratic, for the rates of taxation are the same for the commonest as for the costliest wines; it increases therefore, in geometrical progression as the wealth of the consumers decreases, an inverted progressive tax. It is accordingly a direct provocation to the poisoning of the working classes as a premium on adulterated and spurious wines. It lessens con-

* Nobility.
† Folk deprived of rights.

sumption, since it sets up *octrois* * before the gates of all towns of over 4,000 inhabitants and transforms each town into a foreign country with protective duties against French wine. The big wine merchants, but still more the small ones, the *marchands de vins*, the keepers of wine-shops, whose living directly depends on the consumption of wine, are so many declared enemies of the wine tax. And finally by lessening the consumption the wine tax cuts away the market from production. While it renders the urban workers incapable of paying for wines, it renders the wine growers incapable of selling it. And France has a wine-growing population of about twelve millions. One can, therefore, understand the hate of the people in general, one can, in particular, understand the fanaticism of the peasants against the wine tax. And, in addition, they saw in its restoration no isolated, more or less accidental event. The peasants have a kind of historical tradition of their own, which is handed down from father to son, and in this historical school it is muttered that every government, as long as it wants to dupe the peasants, promises the abolition of the wine tax, and as soon as it has duped the peasants, retains or reintroduces the wine tax. In the wine tax the peasant tests the bouquet of the government, its tendency. The restoration of the wine tax on December 20 meant: Louis Bonaparte is like the others; but he was not like the others; he was a peasant discovery, and in the petitions carrying millions of signatures against the wine tax they took back the votes that they had given a year before to the "nephew of his uncle."

The country folk—over two-thirds of the total French population—consist for the most part of so-called free landed proprietors. The first generation, gratuitously freed by the revolution of 1789 from its feudal burdens, had paid no price for the soil. But the following generations paid, under the form of the price of land, what their semi-serf forefathers had paid in the form of rent, tithes, corvée,† etc. The more, on the one hand, the population grew and the more, on the other hand,

* Local customs offices, at the gates of towns.
† Compulsory, unpaid labor of serfs rendered to feudal lords.

the division of the soil increased—so much the higher became the price of the holdings, for the extent of the demand for them increased with their smallness. But in proportion as the price which the peasant paid for his holding rose, whether he bought it directly or whether he received it as capital from his co-heirs, in this same proportion the indebtedness of the peasant, *i.e.*, the mortgage, necessarily rose. The title to the debt encumbering the land is termed a mortgage, a pawnticket in respect of the land. Just as privileges accumulated on the medieval estate, the mortgages accumulate on the modern tiny holding. On the other hand: under the system of fragmentation of holdings the earth is purely an instrument of production for its proprietors. Now in the same measure as land is divided its fruitfulness diminishes. The application of machinery to the land, the division of labor, the ample means of improving the soil, such as cutting drainage and irrigation channels and the like, become more and more impossible, while the unproductive costs of cultivation increase in the same proportion as the division of the instrument of production itself. All this, apart from whether the possessor of the lot possesses capital or not. But the more the division increases, so much the more the holding with its most utterly wretched inventory forms the entire capital of the small peasant, the more does investment of capital in the land diminish, so much the more does the cotter lack land, money and education for making use of the progress in agriculture, and so much the more does the cultivation of the soil retrogress. Finally, the net proceeds diminish in the same proportion as the gross consumption increases, when the whole family of the peasant is kept back from other occupations through its holding and yet is not enabled to live by it.

In the measure, therefore, that the population and, with it, the division of the land increases, in this same measure the instrument of production, the soil, becomes dearer and its fruitfulness decreases, in this same measure agriculture declines and the peasant becomes loaded with debt. And what was the effect becomes, for its part, the cause. Each generation leaves behind another more deeply in debt; each new generation begins under more unfavorable and more aggravating conditions; mortgaging begets mortgaging, and when it becomes impossible for the peasant to offer his lot as security for new debts, *i.e.*, to encumber it with new mortgages, he falls a victom to usury, and so much the more huge do the usurious sums of interest become.

Thus it came about that the French peasant, in the form of interest on the mortgages encumbering the soil and in the form of interest on the advances made by usury without mortgages, cedes to the capitalist not only ground rent, not only the industrial profit, in a word, not only the whole net profit, but even a part of the wages, and that therefore he has sunk to the level of the Irish tenant farmer—all under the pretense of being a private proprietor.

This process was accelerated in France by the ever growing burden of taxes, by legal expenses called forth in part directly by the formalities themselves, with which French legislation encumbers landed property, in part by the innumerable conflicts over holdings everywhere bounding and crossing each other and in part by the passion for litigation of the peasants, whose enjoyment of property is limited to the fanatical assertion of their fancied property, of their property rights.

According to a statistical statement of 1840 the gross product of French land amounted to 5,237,178,000 francs. Of this, the costs of cultivation come to 3,552,000,000 francs, including the consumption by the tillers of the soil. There remains a net product of 1,685,178,000 francs, from which 550,000,000 have to be deducted for interest on mortgages, 100,000,000 for law officials, 350,000,000 for taxes and 107,000,000 for registration money, stamp money, mortgage fees, etc. There is left one-third of the net product or 538,000,000; when distributed over the population, not 25 francs per head net product. Naturally neither usury not connected with mortgage nor the expenses for lawyers, etc., are included in this calculation.

The condition of the French peasants, when the republic had added new burdens to their old ones, can be understood. It can be seen that their exploitation differs only in form from the exploitation of the industrial proletariat. The exploiter is the same: capital. The individual capitalists exploit the individual peasants through mortgages and usury; the capitalist class exploits the peasant class through the state taxes. The peasant's title to property is the talisman by which capital captivated him hitherto; the pretext under which it set him against the industrial proletariat. Only the fall of capital can raise the peasant; only an anti-capitalist, a proletarian government can break his economic misery, his social degradation. The constitutional republic, that is the dictatorship of his united exploiters; the Social-Democratic, the Red republic, that is the dictatorship of his allies. And the scale rises or falls, according to the votes that the peasant casts into the ballot box. He himself must decide his fate—so spoke the Socialist in pamphlets, almanacs, calendars and leaflets of all kinds. This language became more understandable to him through the counter-writings of the party of order, which, for its part, turned to him and by gross exaggeration, by brutal conception and representation of the intentions and ideas of the Socialists, struck the true peasant note and exceedingly stimulated his lust after forbidden fruit. But most understandable was the language of the actual experiences that the peasant class had from the use of the suffrage, and of the disillusionments that had overwhelmed him, blow upon blow, in revolutionary haste. Revolutions are the locomotives of history.

The gradual revolutionizing of the peasants was manifested by various symptoms. It was already shown in the elections to the Legislative Assembly; it was shown in the state of siege in the five departments bordering Lyons; it was shown a few months after June 13 in the election of a *Montagnard* in place of the former president of the *Chambre introuvable* * by the department of the Gironde; it was shown on December 20, 1849, in the election of a Red in place of a deceased Legitimist deputy in the department of Gard, that lauded land of the Legitimists, the scene of the most frightful infamies committed against the

---

* This is the name given by history to the fanatically ultra-royalist and reactionary Chamber of Deputies elected immediately after the second overthrow of Napoleon in 1815. [Note by Frederick Engels.]

republicans of 1794 and 1795 and the center of the *terreur blanche* * in 1815, where Liberals and Protestants were publically murdered. This revolutionizing of the most stationary class is most clearly evident since the reintroduction of the wine tax. The governmental measures and the laws of January and February, 1850, are directed almost exclusively against the departments and the peasants. The most striking proof of their progress.

The circular of Hautpoul, by which the gendarme was appointed inquisitor of the prefect, of the sub-prefect and, above all, of the mayor, and by which espionage was organized even in the hidden corners of the remotest village communes; the law against the school teachers,[56] by which they, the men of talent, the spokesmen, the educators and interpreters of the peasant class were subjected to the arbitrary power of the prefect, they, the proletarians of the learned class, were chased like hunted beasts from one commune to another; the proposed law against the mayors, by which the Damocles' sword of dismissal hung over their heads, and they, the presidents of the peasant communes, were every moment confronted by the President of the republic and the party of order; the ordinance which transformed the 17 military divisions of France into four pashalics [57] and forced the barracks and the bivouac on the French as the national salons; the education law [58] by which the party of order proclaimed the ignorance and the forcible stupefaction of France as the condition of its own life under the regime of universal suffrage—what were all these laws and measures? Desperate attempts to reconquer the departments and the peasants of the departments for the party of order.

Regarded as repression, wretched methods, that wrung the neck of their own purpose. The big measures, like the retention of the wine tax, of the 45 centimes tax, the scornful rejection of the peasant petitions for the repayment of the milliard, etc., all these legislative thunderbolts struck the peasant class only once, wholesale, from the center; the laws and measures instanced made the attack and the resistance the common topic of the day

* White terror.

in every hut; they inoculated every village with revolution; they localized and peasantized the revolution.

On the other hand, did not these proposals of Bonaparte and their acceptance by the National Assembly prove the unity of the two powers of the constitutional republic, so far as it is a question of repression of anarchy, *i.e.*, of all the classes that rise against the bourgeois dictatorship? Had not Soulouque, directly after his sharp message, assured the Legislative of his devotion to order through the immediately following message of Carlier, that dirty, mean caricature of Fouché,[59] as Louis Bonaparte him-self was the shallow caricature of Napoleon?

The education law shows us the alliance of the young catholic with the old Voltairians. Could the rule of the united bour-geois be anything else but the coalesced despotism of the restora-tion, friendly to the Jesuits, and the would-be free-thinking July monarchy? Had not the weapons that the one bourgeois faction had distributed among the people against the other fac-tion in their mutual struggle for supremacy, again to be torn from it, the people, since the latter was confronted by their united dictatorship? Nothing has aroused the Paris shopkeeper more than this coquettish exhibition of Jesuitism, not even the rejection of the *concordats à l'amiable*.

Meanwhile the collisions between the different factions of the party of order continued, as well as between Bonaparte and the National Assembly. The National Assembly was far from pleased that Bonaparte, immediately after his *coup d'état*, after appointing his own Bonapartist ministry, summoned before him the disabled soldiers of the monarchy, now appointed prefects, and made their unconstitutional agitation for his re-election as President the condition of their appointment; when Carlier cele-brated his inauguration with the closing of a Legitimist club, or when Bonaparte founded a journal of his own, *Le Napoléon*, which betrayed the secret longings of the President to the public, while his ministers had to deny them from the tribune of the Legislative. The latter was far from pleased by the defiant re-tention of the ministry, notwithstanding its various votes of no confidence; far from pleased by the attempt to win the favor of non-commissioned officers by extra pay of four sous a day and the favor of the proletariat by a plagiarizing of Eugène Sue's *Mystères*,* by an honor loan bank; far from pleased, finally, by the effrontery with which the ministers were made to move the deportation of the remaining June insurgents to Algiers, in order to heap unpopularity on the Legislative *en gros*,† while the President reserved popularity for himself *en détail*, by individual grants of pardon. *Thiers* let fall threatening words about *coups d'état* and *coups de tête*,‡ and the Legislative revenged itself on Bonaparte by rejecting every proposed law which he put forward for his own benefit, and by inquiring with noisy mistrust, in every instance where he made a proposal in the common interest, whether through increase of the executive power he did not aspire to augment the personal power of Bonaparte. In a word, it revenged itself by a conspiracy of contempt.

The Legitimist party, on its side, saw with vexation the more capable Orleanists occupying once more almost all posts and centralization increasing, while it sought its well-being principally in decentralization. And so it was. The counter-revolution centralized violently, *i.e.*, it prepared the mechanism of the revolution. It even centralized the gold and silver of France in the Paris bank through the compulsory quotation of bank notes, and so created the complete war chest for the revolution.

Lastly, the Orleanists saw with vexation the rising principle of legitimacy contrasted with their bastard principle and themselves every moment snubbed and maltreated as the bourgeois *mésalliance* ¶ of a noble spouse.

Little by little we have seen peasants, petty bourgeois, the middle classes in general, stepping alongside the proletariat, driven into open antagonism to the official republic, and treated

---

*Mysteries. Eugene Sue's *Mystères* have been translated into English under the titles, *The Mysteries of Paris* and *The Mysteries of the People*, or *The History of a Proletarian Family Across the Ages*. The latter work in nineteen books, was translated into English by Daniel de Leon.

† As a whole.

‡ Seizure of state power and hasty acts. A pun based on the verbal similarity of the two phrases.

¶ Misalliance.

by it as antagonists. Revolt against bourgeois dictatorship, need of a change in society, adherence to democratic-republican institutions as organs of their movement, grouping round the proletariat as the decisive revolutionary power—these were the common characteristics of the so-called party of Social-Democracy, the party of the Red republic. This party of anarchy, as its opponents christened it, is no less a coalition of different interests than the party of order. From the smallest reform of the old social disorder to the overthrow of the old social order, from bourgeois liberalism to revolutionary terrorism, as wide apart as this lie the extremes that form the starting and final point of the party of "anarchy."

Abolition of the protective duties—socialism! For it strikes at the monopoly of the industrial faction of the party of order. Regulation of the state budget—socialism! For it strikes at the monopoly of the financial faction of the party of order. Free admission of foreign meat and corn—socialism! For it strikes at monopoly of the third faction of the party of order, large landed property. The demands of the free-trade party, *i.e.*, of the most advanced English bourgeois party, appear in France as so many socialist demands. Voltairianism—socialism! For it strikes at the fourth faction of the party of order, the catholic. Freedom of the press, right of association, universal public education—socialism, socialism! They strike at the entire monopoly of the party of order.

So swiftly had the march of the revolution ripened conditions, that the friends of reform of all shades, the most moderate claims of the middle classes, were compelled to group themselves round the banner of the most extreme party of revolution, round the red flag.

Yes, manifold as was the socialism of the different large sections of the party of anarchy, according to the economic conditions and the total revolutionary requirements of their class or fraction of a class arising out of these, in one point it is in harmony: in proclaiming itself as the means of emancipating the proletariat and the emancipation of the latter as its object. Deliberate deception on the part of some; self-deception on the part of the others, who give out the world transformed according to their own needs as the best world for all, as the realization of all revolutionary claims and the abolition of all revolutionary collisions.

Under the somewhat similar sounding, general, socialist phrases of the "party of anarchy," is concealed the socialism of the *National,* of the *Presse* and the *Siècle,* which more or less consistently wants to overthrow the rule of the finance aristocracy and to free industry and trade from their hitherto existing fetters. This is the socialism of industry, of trade and of agriculture, whose rulers in the party of order deny these interests, so far as they no longer coincide with their private monopolies. From this bourgeois socialism, to which, as to every variety of socialism, a section of the workers and petty bourgeois naturally rallies, specific petty-bourgeois socialism, socialism *par excellence,* is distinct. Capital hounds this class chiefly as its creditors, so it demands credit institutions; capital crushes it by competition, so it demands associations supported by the state; capital overwhelms it by concentration, so it demands progressive taxes, limitations on inheritance, taking over of large works by the state, and other measures that forcibly stem the growth of capital. Since it dreams of the peaceful achievement of its socialism—allowing, perhaps, for a second February Revolution lasting a brief day—naturally the coming historical process appears to it as the application of systems, which the thinkers of society, whether in companies or as individual inventors, devise or have devised. Thus they become the eclectics or adepts of the existing socialist systems, of doctrinaire socialism, which was the theoretical expression of the proletariat only so long as it had not yet developed further into a free historical self-movement.

While this utopia, doctrinaire socialism, which subordinates the total movement to one of its moments, which puts in place of common, social production the brainwork of individual pedants and, above all, in fantasy does away with the revolutionary struggle of the classes and its necessities by small conjuring tricks or great sentimentality; while this doctrinaire socialism, which at bottom only idealizes the present society, takes a picture of it without shadows and wants to achieve its ideal against the reality of society; while this socialism passes from the proletariat to the petty bourgeoisie; while the struggle of the different socialist chiefs among themselves sets forth each of the so-called systems as a pretentious adherence to one of the transit points of the social revolution as against another—the proletariat rallies more and more round revolutionary socialism, round communism, for which the bourgeoisie has itself found the name of *Blanqui*. This socialism is the declaration of the permanence of the revolution, the class dictatorship of the revolution, the class dictatorship of the proletariat as the inevitable transit point to the abolition of class differences generally, to the abolition of all the productive relations on which they rest, to the abolition of all the social relations that correspond to these relations of production, to the revolutionizing of all the ideas that result from these social connections.

The scope of this exposition does not permit of developing the subject further.

We have seen that just as in the party of order the finance aristocracy inevitably takes the lead, in the party of "anarchy" the proletariat does so. While the different classes united in a revolutionary league grouped themselves round the proletariat, while the departments became ever more unsafe and the Legislative Assembly itself ever more morose towards the pretensions of the French Soulouque, the long deferred and delayed election of substitutes for the *Montagnards* proscribed after June 13 drew near.

The government, scorned by its foes, maltreated and daily humiliated by its alleged friends, saw only one means of emerging from a repugnant and untenable position—a revolt. A revolt in Paris would have permitted the proclamation of a state of siege in Paris and the departments and thus the control of the elections. On the other hand, the friends of order, in face of a government that had gained victory over anarchy were bound to make concessions, if they did not want to appear as anarchists themselves.

The government set to work. At the beginning of February

1850, provocations of the people by cutting down the trees of liberty.[60] In vain. If the trees of liberty lost their place, it itself lost its head and fell back frightened by its own provocation. The National Assembly, however, received this clumsy attempt at emancipation on the part of Bonaparte with ice-cold mistrust. The removal of the wreaths of *immortelles* from the July column was no more successful.[61] It gave a part of the army an opportunity for revolutionary demonstrations and the National Assembly the occasion for a more or less veiled vote of no confidence in the ministry. In vain the government press threatened the abolition of universal suffrage, the invasion of the Cossacks. In vain was d'Hautpoul's direct challenge issued from the midst of the Legislative to the Left, to betake itself to the streets, and his declaration that the government was ready to receive it. Hautpoul received nothing but a call to order from the President, and the party of order with quiet, malicious joy, allowed a deputy of the Left to mock Bonaparte's usurpatory longings. In vain, finally, was the prophesy of a revolution on February 24. The government caused February 24 to be ignored by the people.

The proletariat did not allow itself to be provoked into a rising, because it was on the point of making a revolution.

Unhindered by the provocations of the government, which only heightened the general irritation against the existing situation, the election committee, wholly under the influence of the workers, put forward three candidates for Paris: *Deflotte*, *Vidal* and *Carnot*. Deflotte was a June deportee, amnestied through one of Bonaparte's popularity-seeking ideas; he was a friend of Blanqui's and had taken part in the attempt of May 15. Vidal, known as a Communist writer through his book *Concerning the Distribution of Wealth*, was formerly secretary to Louis Blanc in the Commission of the Luxembourg. Carnot, son of the man of the Convention who had organized victory, the least compromised member of the National party, Minister for Education in the Provisional Government and the Executive Commission, through his democratic education bill was a living protest against the education law of the Jesuits. These three candidates represented the three allied classes: at the head, the June insurgent, the representative of the revolutionary proletariat; next to him, the doctrinaire Socialist, the representative of the Socialist petty bourgeoisie; finally, the third, the representative of the republican bourgeois party, the democratic formulas of which had gained a socialist significance as against the party of order and had long lost their own significance. This was a general coalition against the bourgeoisie and the government, as in February. But this time the proletariat was at the head of the revolutionary league.

In spite of all efforts the Socialist candidates won. The army itself voted for the June insurgent against its own War Minister, Lahitte. The party of order was thunderstruck. The elections in the departments did not solace them; they gave a majority to the *Montagnards*.

The election of March 10, 1850! It was the revocation of June 1848: the butchers and deporters of the June insurgents returned to the National Assembly, but humbled, in the train of the deported, and with their principles on their lips. It was the revocation of June 13, 1849: the Mountain proscribed by the National Assembly returned to the National Assembly, but as advance trumpeters of the revolution, no longer as its commanders. It was the revocation of December 10: Napoleon had been rejected with his minister Lahitte. The parliamentary history of France knows only one analogy: the rejection of d'Haussy, minister of Charles X, in 1830. Finally, the election of March 10, 1850, was the cancellation of the election of May 13, which had given the party of order a majority. The election of March 10 protested against the majority of May 13. March 10 was a revolution. Behind the ballot papers lay the paving stones.

"The vote of March 10 is war," shouted Ségur d'Aguesseau, one of the most advanced members of the party of order.

With March 10, 1850, the constitutional republic entered a new phase, the phase of its dissolution. The different factions of the majority are again united among themselves and with Bonaparte; they are again the saviors of order; he is again their neutral man. If they remember that they are royalists, it happens only from despair of the possibility of the bourgeois republic; if he remembers that he is President, it happens only because he despairs of remaining President.

At the command of the party of order, Bonaparte answers the election of Deflotte, the June insurgent, by appointing Baroches Minister for Internal Affairs, Baroches, the accuser of Blanqui and Barbès, of Ledru-Rollin and Guinard. The Legislative answers the election of Carnot by adopting the education law, the election of Vidal by suppressing the socialist press. The party of order seeks to blare away its own fears by the trumpet-blasts of its press. "The sword is holy," cries one of its organs; "the defenders of order must take the offensive against the Red party," cries another; "between socialism and society there is a duel to the death, a war without rest or mercy; in this duel of desperation one or the other must go under; if society does not annihilate socialism, socialism will annihilate society," crows a third cock of order. Throw up the barricades of order, the barricades of religion, the barricades of the family! An end must be made of the 127,000 voters of Paris! A Bartholomew's night [62] for the Socialists! And the party of order believes for a moment in its own certainty of victory.

Their organs hold forth most fanatically of all against the "shopkeepers of Paris." The June insurgent of Paris elected as their representative by the shopkeepers of Paris! This means that a second June 1848 is impossible; this means that a second June 13, 1849, is impossible; this means that the moral influence of capital is broken; this means that the bourgeois assembly now represents only the bourgeoisie; this means that large property is lost, because its vassal, small property, seeks its salvation in the camp of the propertyless.

The party of order naturally returns to its inevitable commonplace. "More repression," it cries, "tenfold repression!" But its power of repression has diminished tenfold, while the resistance has increased an hundredfold. Must not the chief instrument of repression, the army, itself be repressed? And the party of order speaks its last word, "The iron ring of suffocating legality must be broken. The constitutional republic is impossible. We must fight with our true weapons; since Febuary 1848 we have fought the revolution with its weapons and on its terrain; we have accepted its institutions; the constitution is a fortress, which safeguards only the besiegers, not the besieged! By smuggling ourselves into holy Ilion in the belly of the Trojan horse, we have, unlike our forefathers, the *Grecs*,* not conquered the hostile town, but made ourselves into prisoners."

The foundation of the constitution, however, is universal suffrage. The abolition of universal suffrage is the last word of the party of order, of bourgeois dictatorship.

On May 24, 1848, on December 20, 1848, on May 13, 1849, and on July 8, 1849, universal suffrage admitted that they were right. On March 10, 1850, universal suffrage admitted that it had itself been wrong. Bourgeois rule as the outcome and result of universal suffrage, as the express act of the sovereign will of the people, that is the meaning of the bourgeois constitution. But from the moment that the content of this suffrage, of this sovereign will, is no longer bourgeois rule, has the constitution any further meaning? Is it not the duty of the bourgeoisie so to regulate the suffrage that it wills the reasonable, its rule? By ever and again putting an end to the existing state power and creating it anew out of itself, does not universal suffrage put an end to all stability, does it not every moment question all the powers that be, does it not annihilate authority, does it not threaten to elevate anarchy itself to authority? After March 10, 1850, who should still doubt it?

By repudiating universal suffrage, with which it had hitherto draped itself and from which it sucked its omnipotence, the bourgeoisie openly confesses, "Our dictatorship has hitherto existed by the will of the people; it must now be consolidated against the will of the people. And, consistently, it seeks its supporters no longer within France, but without, in foreign countries, in an invasion.

With the invasion it, a second Coblenz,[63] which has established

---

* Grecs—play on words: Greeks, but also professional cheats. [Note by Frederick Engels.]

its seat in France itself, rouses all the national passions against it. With the attack on universal suffrage it gives a general pretext for the new revolution, and the revolution required such a pretext. Every particular pretext would divide the factions of the revolutionary league, and give prominence to their differences. The general pretext stuns the semi-revolutionary classes; it permits them to deceive themselves concerning the definite character of the coming revolution, concerning the consequences of their own act. Every revolution requires a banquet question. Universal suffrage is the banquet question of the new revolution.

The bourgeois factions in coalition, however, are already condemned, since they take flight from the only possible form of their united power, from the strongest and most complete form of their class rule, the constitutional republic, back to the subordinate, incomplete, weaker form of monarchy. They resemble that old man who, in order to regain his youthful strength, fetched out his boyhood apparel and sought to torment his withered limbs in it. Their republic had the sole merit of being the hot-house of the revolution.

March 10 bears the inscription: *Après moi le déluge!* After me the deluge!

IV

THE ABOLITION OF UNIVERSAL SUFFRAGE, 1850

(*From Double Number V and VI*)

(The continuation of the three foregoing chapters is found in the *Revue* in the fifth and sixth double number of the *Neue Rheinische Zeitung*, the last to appear. There, after the great commercial crisis that broke out in England in 1847 had first been described and the coming of the political complications on the European Continent to a head in the revolutions of February and March 1848 had been explained by its reactions there, it is then shown how the prosperity of trade and industry, that again set in during the course of 1848 and increased still further in 1849, paralyzed the revolutionary upsurge and made possible the simultaneous victories of the reaction. With special reference to France, it is then said:)*

The same symptoms showed themselves in *France* since 1849 and particularly since the beginning of 1850. The Parisian industries are abundantly employed and the cotton factories of Rouen and Mülhausen are also doing pretty well, although here, as in England, the high prices of the raw material have exercised a retarding influence. The development of prosperity in France was, in addition, especially advanced by the comprehensive tariff reform in Spain and by the reduction of the duties on various luxury articles in Mexico; the export of French commodities to both markets has considerably increased. The growth of capital in France led to a series of speculations, for which the exploitation of the Californian gold mines on a large scale served as a pretext. A swarm of companies sprang up, the low denomination of whose shares and whose socialist-colored prospectuses appeal directly to the purses of the petty bourgeois and

---

* Introductory note by Frederick Engels.

the workers, but which all and sundry result in that sheer swindling which is characteristic of the French and Chinese alone. One of these companies is even patronized directly by the government. The import duties in France during the first nine months of 1848 amounted to 63,000,000 francs, of 1849 to 95,000,000 francs and of 1850 to 93,000,000 francs. Moreover, in the month of September 1850 they again rose by more than a million compared with the same month of 1849. Exports had also risen in 1849 and still more in 1850.

The most striking proof of restored prosperity is the reintroduction of cash payments by the bank by the law of September 6, 1850. On March 15, 1848, the bank was authorized to suspend its cash payments. Its note circulation, including the provincial banks, amounted at that time to 373,000,000 francs (£14,920,000 sterling). On November 2, 1849, this circulation amounted to 482,000,000 francs or £19,280,000 sterling, an increase of £4,360,000 sterling, and on September 2, 1850, to 496,000,000 francs or £19,840,000 sterling, an increase of some £5,000,000 sterling. This was not accompanied by any deprecia tion of the notes; on the contrary the increased circulation of the notes was accompanied by the steadily increasing accumula tion of gold and silver in the cellars of the bank, so that in the summer of 1850 its metallic reserve amounted to about £14,000,000 sterling, an unprecedented sum in France. That the bank was thus placed in a position to increase its circulation and therewith its active capital by 123,000,000 francs or £5,- 000,000 sterling is a striking proof of the correctness of our assertion in the earlier number that the finance aristocracy has not only not been overthrown by the revolution, but has even been strengthened. This result becomes still more evident from the following survey of the French bank legislation of the last few years. On June 10, 1847, the bank was authorized to issue notes of 200 francs; hitherto the smallest note had been one of 500 francs. A decree of March 15, 1848, declared the notes of the Bank of France legal tender and relieved the Bank of the obligation of redeeming them in cash. Its note issue was limited to 350,000,000 francs. It was simultaneously authorized to issue notes of 100 francs. A decree of April 27 prescribed the merging of the departmental banks in the Bank of France; another decree of May 2, 1848, increased the latter's note issue to 422,000,000 francs. A decree of December 22, 1849, raised the maximum of the note issue to 525,000,000 francs. Finally, the law of September 6, 1850, re-introduced the exchangeability of notes for gold. These facts, the continual increase in the circulation, the concentration of the whole of French credit in the hands of the Bank and the accumulation of all French gold and silver in the Bank vaults, led Mr. Proudhon [64] to the conclusion that the Bank must now shed its old snakeskin and metamorphose itself into a Proudhonist people's bank. He did not even need to know the history of the English Bank restriction from 1797-1819; he only needed to direct his glance across the Channel to see that this fact, for him unprecedented in the history of bourgeois society, was nothing more than a very normal bourgeois event that now only occurred in France for the first time. One sees that the alleged revolutionary theoreticians who, after the Provisional Government, talked big in Paris, were just as ignorant of the nature and the results of the measures taken, as the gentlemen of the Provisional Government themselves. In spite of the industrial and commercial prosperity that France momentarily enjoys, the mass of the people, the twenty-five million peasants, labor under a state of great depression. The good harvests of the last few years have forced the prices of corn much lower than in England, and the position of the peasants in such circumstances, in debt, sucked dry by usury and crushed by taxes, can only be anything but brilliant. The history of the last three years has, however, provided sufficient proof that this class of the population is capable of absolutely no revolutionary initiative.

Just as the period of crisis occurs later on the Continent than in England, so does that of prosperity. The original process always takes place in England; she is the demiurge of the bourgeois cosmos. On the Continent, the different phases of the cycle through which bourgeois society is ever speeding anew, occur in secondary and tertiary form. First, the Continent exported incomparably more to England than to any other country. This export to England, however, in turn depends on the position of England, particularly with regard to the overseas market. Then England exports to the overseas lands incomparably more than the entire Continent, so that the quantity of Continental exports to these lands is always dependent on England's overseas exports in each case. If, therefore, the crises first produce revolutions on the Continent, the foundation for these is, nevertheless, always laid in England. Violent outbreaks must naturally occur earlier in the extremities of the bourgeois body than in its heart, since here the possibility of adjustment is greater than there. On the other hand, the degree to which the Continental revolutions react on England, is at the same time the thermometer on which is indicated how far these revolutions really call in question the bourgeois conditions of life, or how far they only hit their political formations.

With this general prosperity, in which the productive forces of bourgeois society develop as luxuriantly as is at all possible within bourgeois relationships, there can be no talk of a real revolution. Such a revolution is only possible in the periods when these two factors, the modern productive forces and the bourgeois production forms, come in collision with one another. The various quarrels in which the representatives of the individual factions of the Continental party of order now indulge and mutually compromise themselves, far from providing the occasion for new revolutions, are, on the contrary, only possible because the basis of the relationships is momentarily so secure, and (what the reaction does not know) so bourgeois. From it all attempts of the reaction to hold up bourgeois development will rebound just as lightly as all moral indignation and all enthusiastic proclamations of the democrats. A new revolution is only possible in consequence of a new crisis. It is, however, also just as certain as this.

Let us now turn to France.

The victory that the people, in conjunction with the petty bourgeois, had won in the elections of March 10, was annulled by it itself when it provoked the new election of April 28. As well as in Paris, Vidal was also elected in the Lower Rhine. The Paris Committee, in which the Mountain and the petty bourgeoisie were strongly represented, induced him to accept for the Lower Rhine. The victory of March 10 ceased to be a decisive one; the date of the decision was once more postponed; the tension of the people was relaxed; it became accustomed to legal triumphs instead of the revolutionary ones. The revolutionary meaning of March 10, the rehabilitation of the June insurrection, was finally completely annihilated by the candidature of Eugène Sue, the sentimental petty bourgeois social-fantast, which the proletariat could at best accept as a joke to please the *grisettes*. As against this well-meaning candidature, the party of order, emboldened by the vacillating policy of its opponent, put up a candidate who was to represent the June victory. This comic candidate was the Spartan *paterfamilias*,* Leclerc, from whose person the heroic armor was torn piece by piece by the press, and who also experienced a brilliant defeat in the election. The new election victory on April 28 made the Mountain and the petty bourgeoisie overconfident. They already exulted in the thought of being able to arrive at the goal of their wishes in a purely legal way and without again pushing the proletariat into the foreground through a new revolution; they reckoned positively on bringing Ledru-Rollin into the presidential chair, and a majority of the *Montagnards* into the Assembly through universal suffrage in the new elections of 1852. The party of order, rendered perfectly certain by the prospective elections, by the candidature of Sue and by the mood of the Mountain and the petty bourgeoisie that the latter were resolved to remain quiet under all circumstances, answered the two election victories with the election law which abolished universal suffrage.

The government took good care not to make this legislative proposal on its own responsibility. It made an apparent concession to the majority by entrusting the working out of the bill to the high dignitaries of this majority, the seventeen burgraves. Therefore, it was not the government that proposed the repeal

* Head of the family.

of universal suffrage to the Assembly; the majority of the Assembly proposed it to itself.

On May 8, the project was brought into the Chamber. The entire social-democratic press rose as one man in order to preach to the people dignified bearing, *calme majestueux*,* passivity and trust in its representatives. Every article of these journals was a confession that a revolution must, above all, annihilate the so-called revolutionary press and that, therefore, it was now a question of their self-preservation. The alleged revolutionary press betrayed its whole secret. It signed its own death warrant.

On May 21, the Mountain put the preliminary question to debate and moved the rejection of the whole project because it violated the constitution. The party of order answered that the constitution would be violated if it were necessary; there was, however, no need for this at present, because the constitution was capable of every interpretation, and because the majority was alone competent to decide on the correct interpretation. To the unbridled, savage attacks of Thiers and Montalembert the Mountain opposed a decorous and civilized humanism. It took its stand on the ground of law; the party of order referred it to the ground on which the law grows, to bourgeois property. The Mountain whimpered: Did they really want, then, to conjure up revolutions by main force? The party of order replied: One would await them.

On May 22, the preliminary question was settled by 462 votes to 227. The same men who had proved with such solemn profundity that the National Assembly and every individual deputy would abdicate if they dismissed the people, their mandator, stuck to their seats, now suddenly sought to let the country act, through petitions at that, instead of themselves, and still sat there unmoved when, on May 31, the law passed brilliantly. They sought to revenge themselves through a protest, in which they recorded their innocence of the rape of the constitution, a protest which they did not even set down openly, but smuggled into the President's pocket from behind.

* Majestic calm.

An army of 150,000 men in Paris, the long deferment of the decision, the peaceful attitude of the press, the pusillanimity of the Mountain and the newly elected representatives, the majestic calm of the petty bourgeois, but, above all, the commercial and industrial prosperity, prevented any attempt at revolution on the part of the proletariat.

Universal suffrage had fulfilled its mission. The majority of the people had passed through the school of development, which is all that universal suffrage can serve for in a revolutionary period. It had to be set aside by a revolution or by the reaction.

The Mountain developed a still greater display of energy on an occasion that soon afterwards arose. The War Minister, d'Hautpoul, termed the February Revolution from the tribune a disastrous catastrophe. The orators of the Mountain, who, as always, distinguished themselves by morally indignant uproar, were not allowed to speak by the President, Dupin. Girardin proposed to the Mountain that it should walk out at once *en masse*. Result: the Mountain remained seated, but Girardin was cast out from its midst as unworthy.

The election law still needed one thing to complete it, a new press law. This was not long in coming. A proposal of the government, made many times more drastic by amendments of the party of order, increased the caution money, put an extra stamp on feuilleton novels (answer to the election of Eugène Sue), taxed all publications appearing in weekly or monthly parts up to a certain number of sheets and finally provided that every article of a journal must bear the signature of the author. The provisions concerning the caution money killed the so-called revolutionary press; the people regarded its extinction as satisfaction for the abolition of universal suffrage. However, neither the tendency nor the effect of the new law extended only to this section of the press. As long as the newspaper press was anonymous, it appeared as the organ of a numberless and nameless public opinion; it was the third power in the state. Through the signature of every article, a newspaper became a mere collection of literary contributions from more or less known individuals. Every article sank to the level of an advertisement.

Hitherto the newspapers had circulated as the paper money of public opinion; now they were resolved into more or less bad *solo* bills, whose worth and circulation depended on the credit not only of the drawer but also of the endorser. The press of the party of order had not only incited for the repeal of universal suffrage but also for the most extreme measures against the bad press. However, in its sinister anonymity even the good press was irksome to the party of order and still more to its individual and provincial representatives. As for itself it still demanded only the paid writer, with name, address and description. In vain the good press bemoaned the ingratitude with which its services were rewarded. The law went through; the provision concerning the giving of names hit it hardest of all. The names of republican journalists were pretty well known; but the respectable firms of the *Journal des Débats*, the *Assemblée Nationale*, the *Constitutionnelle*, etc., etc., cut a sorry figure in their high protestations of state wisdom, when the mysterious company all at once disintegrated into purchasable penny-a-liners of long practice, who had defended all possible causes for cash, like Granier de Cassagnac, or into old milksops who called themselves statesmen, like Capefigue, or into coquettish fops, like Mr. Lemoinne of the *Débats*.

In the debate on the press law the Mountain had already sunk to such a level of moral degeneracy that it had to confine itself to applauding the brilliant tirades of an old notability of Louis Philippe's time, Mr. Victor Hugo.

With the election law and the press law the revolutionary and democratic party steps off the official stage. Before their departure home, shortly after the end of the session, both factions of the Mountain, the socialist democrats and the democratic socialists, issued two manifestos, two *testimonia pauperitatis*,* in which they proved that if neither power nor success were on their side, nevertheless they had ever been on the side of eternal justice and all the other eternal truths.

Let us now consider the party of order. The *N. Rh. Z.* had said (Number III, p. 16):

* Certificates of poverty.

As against the hankerings for restoration on the part of the united Orleanists and Legitimists, Bonaparte represents the title of his actual power, the republic. As against the hankerings for restoration on the part of Bonaparte, the party of order represents the title of its common rule: the republic. As against the Orleanists, the Legitimists and as against the Legitimists, the Orleanists represent the *status quo:* the republic. All these factions of the party of order, each of which has its own king and its own restoration *in petto*, mutually assert, as against their rivals' desires for usurpation and elevation, the common rule of the bourgeoisie, the form in which the particular claims remain neutralized and reserved: the republic. ...And Thiers spoke more truly than he suspected, when he said: We, the royalists, are the true pillars of the constituent republic.

This comedy of the *républicains malgré eux,** of antipathy to the *status quo* and constant consolidation of it; the incessant friction between Bonaparte and the National Assembly; the ever renewed threat of the party of order to split into its single component parts, and the ever repeated reunion of its factions; the attempt of each faction to transform each victory over the common foe into a defeat for its temporary allies; the mutual petty jealousy, chicanery, harassment, the tireless drawing of swords that ever and again ends with a *baiser-Lamourette* 65— this whole unedifying comedy of errors never developed more classically than during the last six months.

The party of order regarded the election law at the same time as a victory over Bonaparte. Had not the government abdicated when it handed over the editing of and responsibility for its own proposal to the Commission of seventeen? And did not the chief strength of Bonaparte as against the Assembly lie in the fact that he was the chosen of six millions?—Bonaparte, for his part, treated the election law as a concession to the Assembly, with which he had purchased harmony between the legislative and executive powers. As reward, the vulgar adventurer demanded an increase of three millions in his civil list. Dared the National Assembly enter a conflict with the executive at a moment when it had excommunicated the great majority of Frenchmen? It was roused to anger; it appeared

* Republicans in spite of themselves.

to want to go to extremes; its Commission rejected the motion; the Bonapartist press threatened, and referred to the disinherited people, deprived of is franchise; numerous noisy attempts at an arrangement took place, and the Assembly finally gave way in fact, but at the same time revenged itself in principle. Instead of increasing the civil list in principle by three millions per annum, it granted him an accommodation of 2,160,000 francs. Not satisfied with this, it made the concession only after it had been supported by Changarnier, the general of the party of order and the protector thrust upon Bonaparte. Really, therefore, it granted the two millions not to Bonaparte, but to Changarnier.

This present, thrown to him *de mauvaise grâce*,* was accepted by Bonaparte quite in the spirit of the donor. The Bonapartist press blustered anew against the National Assembly. When, now in the debate on the press law, the amendment was made on the signing of names, which, in turn, was directed especially against the less important papers—the representatives of the private interests of Bonaparte, the principal Bonapartist paper, the *Pouvoir*, published an open and vehement attack on the National Assembly. The ministers had to disavow the paper before the National Assembly; the chief editor of the *Pouvoir* was summoned before the bar of the National Assembly and sentenced to pay the highest fine, 5,000 francs. Next day the *Pouvoir* published a much more insolent article against the Assembly, and, as the revenge of the government, the public prosecutor promptly prosecuted a number of Legitimist journals for violating the constitution.

Finally there came the question of proroguing the Chamber. Bonaparte desired this in order to be able to operate unhindered by the Assembly. The party of order desired it partly for the purpose of carrying on their factional intrigues, partly for the pursuit of the private interests of individual deputies. Both needed it in order to consolidate and push further the victories of the reaction in the provinces. The Assembly therefore adjourned from August 11 until November 11. Since, however,

* With bad grace.

Bonaparte in no way concealed that his own concern was to get rid of the irksome surveillance of the National Assembly, the Assembly imprinted on the vote of confidence itself the stamp of want of confidence in the President. All Bonapartists were kept off the permanent commission of twenty-eight members, who persevered during the recess as guardians of the virtue of the republic. In their stead, some republicans of the *Siècle* and the *National* were actually elected to it, in order to prove to the President the attachment of the majority to the constitutional republic.

Shortly before and, especially, immediately after the proroguing of the Chamber, the two big factions of the party of order, the Orleanists and the Legitimists, appeared to want to be reconciled, and that by a merger of the two royal houses under whose flags they fight. The papers were full of reconciliation proposals that had been discussed at the sick bed of Louis Philippe at St. Leonards, when the death of Louis Philippe suddenly simplified the situation. Louis Philippe was the usurper; Henry V, the dispossessed; the Count of Paris, on the other hand, owing to the childlessness of Henry V, his lawful heir to the throne. Every objection to the fusion of the two dynastic interests was now removed. But now, precisely, the two factions of the bourgeoisie first discovered that it was not zeal for a definite royal house that divided them, but that it was rather their divided class interests that kept the two dynasties apart. The Legitimists who had made a pilgrimage to the residence of Henry V at Wiesbaden just as their competitors had to St. Leonards, received there the news of Louis Philippe's death. Forthwith they formed a ministry *in partibus infidelium*,* which consisted mostly of members of that commission of guardians of the virtue of the republic and which, on the occasion of a squabble taking place in the bosom of the party, came out with the most outspoken proclamation of right by the grace of God. The Orleanists rejoiced over the compromising scandal that this manifesto called forth in the press, and did not conceal for a moment their open enmity to the Legitimists.

* In the midst of the infidels. See footnote, p. 13.

During the adjournment of the National Assembly, the meeting of the councils of the departments took place. The majority of them declared themselves for a more or less qualified revision of the constitution, *i.e.*, they declared themselves for a monarchist restoration not strictly defined, for a "solution," and confessed at the same time that they were too incompetent and too cowardly to find this solution. The Bonapartist faction construed this desire for revision in the sense of a prolongation of Bonaparte's Presidency.

The constitutional solution, the retirement of Bonaparte in May 1852, the simultaneous election of a new President by all the electors of the land, the revision of the constitution by a Chamber of revision in the first months of the new Presidency, is utterly inadmissible for the ruling class. The day of the new presidential election would be the day of the *rendezvous* for all the hostile parties, the Legitimists, the Orleanists, the bourgeois republicans, the revolutionaries. It must come to a violent decision between the different factions. Even if the party of order should succeed in uniting round the candidature of a neutral person outside the dynastic families, he would still be opposed by Bonaparte. In its struggle with the people, the party of order is compelled constantly to increase the power of the executive. Every increase of the executive's power increases the power of its bearer, Bonaparte. In the same measure, therefore, as the party of order strengthens its joint might, it strengthens the fighting resources of Bonaparte's dynastic pretensions, it strengthens his chance of frustrating the constitutional solution by force on the day of the decision. He will then have, as against the party of order, no more scruples about the one pillar of the constitution than the party had, as against the people, about the other pillar in the matter of the election law. As against the Assembly, he would seemingly appeal even to universal suffrage. In a word, the constitutional solution questions the entire political *status quo*, and behind the jeopardizing of the *status quo*, the bourgeois sees chaos, anarchy, civil war. He sees his purchases and sales, his bills of exchange, his marriages, his legal contracts, his mortgages, his ground rents, house rents, profits, all his contracts and sources of gain called in question on the first Sunday in May 1852 and he cannot expose himself to this risk. Behind the jeopardizing of the political *status quo* lurks the danger of the collapse of the entire bourgeois society. The only possible solution in the bourgeois sense is the postponement of the solution. It can only save the constitutional republic by a violation of the constitution, by the prolongation of the power of the President. This is also the last word of the press of order, after the protracted and thoughtful debates on the "solutions," to which it devoted itself after the session of the general councils. The high and mighty party of order thus finds itself, to its shame, compelled to take seriously the ridiculous, commonplace and, to it, odious person of the pseudo-Bonaparte.

This dirty figure likewise deceived himself concerning the causes that clothed him more and more with the character of the indispensable man. While his party had sufficient insight to ascribe the growing importance of Bonaparte to the circumstances, he believed that he owed it solely to the magic power of his name and his continual caricaturing of Napoleon. He became daily more enterprising. To the pilgrimages to St. Leonards and Wiesbaden he opposed his round tours of France. The Bonapartists had so little faith in the magical effect of his personality that they sent with him everywhere as *claquers* people from the Society of December the Tenth,[66] that organization of the Paris lumpenproletariat, packed *en masse* into railway trains and post-chaises. They put speeches into the mouth of their marionette which, according to the reception in the different towns, proclaimed republican resignation or perennial tenacity as the keynote of the President's policy. In spite of all the maneuvers these journeys were anything but triumphant processions.

When Bonaparte believed he had thus enthused the people, he set out to win the army. He caused great reviews to be held on the plain of Satori near Versailles, at which he sought to buy the soldiers with garlic sausages, champagne and cigars. If the genuine Napoleon, amid the hardships of his campaigns of conquest, knew how to encourage his weary soldiers with outbursts of patriarchal familiarity, the pseudo-Napoleon believed it was in gratitude that the troops shouted: *Vive Napoléon, vive le saucisson!* that is, long live the sausage, long live the buffoon! *

These reviews led to the outbreak of the long suppressed dissension between Bonaparte and his War Minister, d'Hautpoul, on the one hand, and Changarnier, on the other. In Changarnier, the party of order had found its real neutral man, in whose case there could be no question of his own dynastic claims. It had designated him as Bonaparte's successor. In addition, Changarnier had become the general of the party of order through his conduct on January 29 and June 13, 1849, the modern Alexander, whose brutal intervention had, in the eyes of the frightened bourgeois, cut the Gordian knot of the revolution. At bottom just as ridiculous as Bonaparte, he had thus become a power in the very cheapest manner and was set up by the National Assembly against the President to watch over him. He himself coquetted, for example, in the matter of the grant, with the protection that he gave Bonaparte, and rose up even more overpoweringly against him and the ministers. When, on the occasion of the election law, an insurrection was expected, he forbade his officers to take any orders whatever from the War Minister or the President. The press was further instrumental in magnifying the figure of Changarnier. With the complete absence of great personalities, the party of order naturally found itself compelled to endow with the strength lacking in its class as a whole a single individual and so puff up this individual to a prodigy. Thus arose the myth of Changarnier, the "bulwark of society." The arrogant charlatanry, the secretive officiousness with which Changarnier condescended to carry the world on his shoulders, forms the most ridiculous contrast to the events during and after the Satori review, which irrefutably proved that it needed only a stroke of the pen by Bonaparte, the infinitely little, to bring this fantastic offspring of bourgeois fear, the colossus Changarnier, back to the dimen-

* A play on words. Sausage in German—*Wurst;* buffoon—*Hanswurst.*
Es lebe die Wurst, es lebe der Hanswurst!

sions of mediocrity, and transform him, society's heroic savior, into a pensioned general.

Bonaparte had for some time revenged himself on Changarnier by provoking the War Minister to disputes in matters of discipline with the irksome protector. The last review at Satori finally brought the old animosity to a climax. The constitutional indignation of Changarnier knew no bounds when he saw the cavalry regiments file past with the unconstitutional cry: *vive l'Empereur!* Bonaparte, in order to forestall any unpleasant debate on this cry in the coming session of the Chamber, removed the War Minister d'Hautpoul, by appointing him Governor of Algiers. In his place he put a reliable old general of the time of the Emperor, one who was fully a match for Changarnier in brutality. But so that the dismissal of d'Hautpoul might not appear as a concession to Changarnier, he simultaneously transferred General Neumayer, the right hand of the great savior of society, from Paris to Nantes. It had been Neumayer, who at the last review had induced the whole of the infantry to file past the successor of Napoleon in icy silence. Changarnier, himself hit in the person of Neumayer, protested and threatened. To no purpose. After two days' negotiations, the decree for transferring Neumayer appeared in the *Moniteur,* and there was nothing left for the hero of order but to submit to discipline or resign.

The struggle of Bonaparte with Changarnier is the continuation of his struggle with the party of order. The re-opening of the National Assembly on November 11 therefore takes place under threatening auspices. It will be a storm in a tea cup. In essence the old game must go on. Meanwhile the majority of the party of order will, despite the clamor of the sticklers on principle of its different factions, be compelled to prolong the power of the President. Similarly, Bonaparte, already humbled by lack of money, will, despite all preliminary protestations, accept this prolongation of power as simply delegated to him from the hands of the National Assembly. Thus the solution is post-- poned; the *status quo* continued; one faction of the party of order compromised, weakened, made impossible by the other;

the repression of the common enemy, the mass of the nation, extended and exhausted, until the economic relations themselves have again reached the point of development where a new explosion blows into the air all the squabbling parties with their constitutional republic.

For the peace of mind of the bourgeois, moreover, it must be said that the scandal between Bonaparte and the party of order has the result of ruining a multitude of small capitalists on the Bourse and putting their possessions in the pockets of the big Bourse wolves.

EXPLANATORY NOTES

EXPLANATORY NOTES

1. This introduction of Engels to *The Class Struggles in France* has a history of its own. On its publication in the Berlin *Vorwärts* in 1895, the text was subjected to such cuts that Engels' arguments were essentially distorted. Engels wrote about this to Lafargue on April 3, 1895, as follows:

"L. [Engels has in mind Wilhelm Liebknecht] has played a pretty trick on me. From my *Introduction* to the articles of Marx about France of 1848 to 1850, he has taken everything which could serve to defend *the tactics of peace and anti-violence* at all costs, which he has found it convenient to preach for some time past, especially at the present moment when the Exceptional Law is being prepared in Berlin. But I recommend these tactics only for the *Germany of the present time,* and that too *with essential reservations.* In France, Belgium, Italy and Austria it is impossible to follow this tactic in its entirety and in Germany it can become unsuitable tomorrow."

Indignant at the unceremonious "editorial" work performed on his *Introduction,* Engels also wrote to Kautsky on April 1, 1895:

"To my astonishment I see today in *Vorwärts* an extract from my *Introduction* printed without my knowledge and dealt with in such a fashion that I appear as a peaceful worshiper of legality *quand même* [at all costs]. I am therefore so much the more glad that the whole is appearing in its entirety in the *Neue Zeit* so that this *disgraceful impression* will be wiped out.

"I shall very definitely express my opinion about this to Liebknecht and also to those, whoever they may be, who have given him this opportunity to distort my opinion."

It is not an accident that German Social-Democracy did not find time, for almost forty years, to publish the accurate text of Engels' "Introduction." In his revisionist *Prerequisites of Socialism,* Eduard Bernstein attempted to represent the distorted "Introduction" published in the *Vorwärts* as a "political testament" in which Engels is supposed to have broken with his revolutionary past. The accurate text was published for the first time by the Marx-Engels-Lenin Institute which is in possession of the complete text of Engels' "Introduction."

2. The Revolution of 1848 began in France on February 24, in Germany during March (in Vienna on March 13, in Berlin on March 18).

3. On the feudal bourgeoisie and petty-bourgeois socialism see *The Communist Manifesto* of Marx and Engels, chap. III.

4. The extensive estate presented to the German Chancellor Bismarck.

5. The parties referred to are the *Legitimists,* the supporters of the "legitimate" monarchy of the Bourbons who were in power in France up to the Revolution of 1789 and also during the epoch of the Restoration (1815-30), and the *Orleanists,* the supporters of the Orleans dynasty who came to power during the July Revolution of 1830 and who were overthrown by the Revo-

lution of 1848. The first represented the interests of the big landowners, the second those of the bankers and financial aristocracy.

6. During the period of Napoleon III, France took part in the Crimean War (1854-56), carried on war with Austria on account of Italy (1859), organized an expedition into Syria (1860), took part together with England in the war against China, conquered Cambodia (Indo-China) in 1863, took part in the Mexican expedition and finally in 1870 made war against Prussia.

7. As a result of the victories over France during the Franco-Prussian War of 1870-71 there arose the German Empire from which, however, Austria was excluded. (Hence the term "the Little German Empire.") The defeat of Napoleon III gave an impulse to the revolution in France which overthrew Louis Bonaparte and which led, on September 4, 1870, to the establishment of the republic.

8. The Paris Commune was suppressed with unprecedented ferocity during May 1871 (May 21-28).

9. Universal suffrage was introduced by Bismarck in 1866 for the elections to the Reichstag of the United German Empire.

10. The reference is to the program of the French Labor Party drawn up by Guesde and Paul Lafargue under the immediate guidance of Marx.

11. The *Garde Nationale* was the name given to the civil militia in France which was first set up during the time of the Great French Revolution (1789). During the epoch of the July Monarchy (1830-48) the National Guard consisted of various bourgeois elements.

12. On September 4, 1870, the government of Louis Bonaparte was overthrown and the republic proclaimed, and on October 31 of the same year there took place the unsuccessful attempt of the Blanquists to make an insurrection against the government of national defense.

13. Frederick the Great, King of Prussia (1712-86).

14. At the battle of Wagram in 1809 Napoleon I defeated the Austrian army, while at Waterloo on July 18 he suffered a decisive defeat at the hands of the allied armies (the Austrian, Prussian, British, etc.).

15. The draft of the new law against the Socialists was introduced in the Reichstag on December 5, 1894; the bill was handed over to a commission which discussed it up to April 25, 1895.

16. After the victory of the July revolution, the Duke of Orleans (Louis Philippe) was proclaimed "vice-regent" and afterwards King. The temporary government established after the overthrow of Charles X sat in the town hall.

17. On June 5, 1832, took place the uprising in Paris organized by the *Society of the Friends of the People* and other revolutionary societies. The occasion was furnished by the burial of General Lamarck, the leader of the republican group in the Chamber of Deputies. The revolutionary organizations proposed to arrange merely a demonstration but it ended in bloodshed. When the demonstrators brought out the Red flag with the inscription "liberty or death," the troops hurled themselves upon them. Barricades were thrown up, the last of which were only destroyed by cannon fire on the evening of June 6.

On April 9, 1834, a new rising of the Lyons workers broke out (the first took place in 1831). The immediate cause was the verdict pronounced by the court against certain workers as instigators of the struggle for increased wages. After a stubborn and bloody struggle which lasted several days, the rising ended in a defeat for the workers.

On May 12, 1839, there took place an unsuccessful attempt at insurrection by the Blanquist Society of the Seasons. It is dealt with in the pamphlet of Engels *On the History of the Communist League.*

18. The Constituent Assembly sat from May 4, 1848, to May 26, 1849, and the Legislative Assembly from May 28, 1849, to December 2, 1851.

19. The chief town in the Department of the Gironde, one of the centers of French wine-growing.

20. Literally "legal country." This designation was applied during the period of the July Monarchy to the possessing minority who had electoral rights in contradistinction to the wide masses of the population who were deprived of electoral rights.

21. Robert Macaire is the type of an artful dodger in the comedy of Benjamin Antier and F. Lemaître, entitled *Robert and Bertrand* (1834).

22. The term was applied in France to cafés of a doubtful character.

23. The Holy Alliance was the alliance of the counter-revolutionary monarchies of Russia, Austria and Prussia, founded in 1815.

24. In 1847 in Buzançais, in connection with the incipient famine, two rich landowners were killed by an excited crowd as grain usurers; five persons were executed on account of this murder.

25. To all demands for electoral reform the minister Guizot answered, "Get rich and you will become electors."

26. Louis Philippe, frightened by the popular uprising which was beginning, dismissed the Guizot ministry on February 23 and on the morning of the 24th appointed the ministry of Odilon Barrot.

27. The organ of the bourgeois republican opposition, founded by Thiers in 1830.

28. The party of the period of the July Monarchy, headed by Odilon Barrot. It represented the interests of the bourgeoisie which was dissatisfied with the political domination of the financial aristocracy.

29. At the time of the July Revolution in 1830, the masses of the people who were fighting on the barricades and demanding the introduction of universal suffrage, the republic and the convening of the Constituent Assembly, were not able to exhibit such a degree of organization as the bourgeoisie. The financial aristocracy and bankers utilized the victory of the people to call to the throne the Duke of Orleans (Louis Philippe).

30. The old monarchist newspaper.

31. By agreeing to the establishment of the Luxembourg Commission Louis Blanc assisted the maneuver of the bourgeoisie which was playing to gain time by means of empty promises. In entering the government, Louis Blanc showed himself to be an appendage of the bourgeoisie, an obedient tool in its hands. Lenin drew a parallel between the role of Louis Blanc in the Revolution of 1848 and the role of the Mensheviks and the Socialist-Revolutionaries in 1917 in his article "In Louis Blanc's Footsteps": "The French Socialist, Louis Blanc, gained deplorable fame in the Revolution of 1848 by changing from the position of the class struggle to the position of petty-bourgeois illusions, adorned with would-be 'socialist' phraseology, but in reality tending to strengthen the influ-

ence of the bourgeoisie over the proletariat. Louis Blanc expected to receive aid from the bourgeoisie; he hoped, and aroused hopes in others, that the bourgeoisie *could* aid the workers in the matter of 'organization of labor'—this vague term having been supposed to express a 'socialist' tendency." (Lenin, *Collected Works*, English edition, Vol. XX, Book I, p. 111.) The example of Louis Blanc afterwards found numerous followers. The isolated examples of the entry of Socialists into bourgeois governments was converted by the Second International after the war into a regular practice. The parties of the Second International sent their representatives into bourgeois governments in order by the aid of these "socialist" lackeys to mask the dictatorship of capitalism.

32. The economic policy of the July Monarchy was distinguished by a system of extreme protectionism. The import of pig iron, iron and steel manufactures, textiles, paper, etc., was subject to such high duties that they practically could not reach the French market.

33. A struggle arose on the question of the flag of the French Republic. The workers demanded that the flag of the republic should include the Red flag. The bourgeoisie defended the tricolor. The struggle ended in the typical compromise of the February days; the flag of the republic was declared to be the tricolor with a red rosette.

34. Marx had in mind the March revolutions of 1848 in Prussia and Austria, the uprising of the Poles of 1848 and the revolutions of 1848 in Hungary and Italy.

35. Under the influence of the 1848 Revolution in France there took place in England a new and final upsurge of the Chartist movement.

36. A contemptuous nickname applied by the French landowners to the peasants.

37. Compare Lenin's remark:

"The issue in France in 1789 was the overthrow of absolutism and nobility. On the then existing level of economic and political development the bourgeoisie believed in the harmony of interests. It was not afraid to lose its domination, and therefore it agreed to a union with the peasantry.... The issue in 1848 was the overthrow of the bourgeoisie by the proletariat. The latter failed to attract the petty bourgeoisie, whose betrayal caused the defeat of the revolution." (Lenin, "Two Lines of the Revolution," *Collected Works*, English edition, Vol. XVIII, pp. 359-60.)

38. In connection with the events of May 15, 1848, Barbès, Albert, Raspail, Sobrier, and within a few days Blanqui also, were arrested and cast into the Vincennes prison.

39. ¯n September 1831 the Minister of Foreign Affairs Sebastiani, in discussing the policy of the government in relation to the insurrection in Poland which had just been suppressed by the Russian autocracy, uttered the notorious phrase "Order reigns in Warsaw."

40. See the statement of Stalin:

"Leninism has proved, and the imperialist war and the revolution in Russia have confirmed it, that the national question can be solved only in connection with and on the basis of the proletarian revolution, that the path to victory of the revolution in the West proceeds through the revolutionary alliance with the movement for liberation of the colonies and dependent countries against imperialism. The national question is part of the general question of the proletarian revolution, part of the question of the dictatorship of the proletariat." (Joseph Stalin, *Foundations of Leninism*, pp. 75-76.)

41. The party of the Mountain (the *Montagnards*) was the name applied during the time of the 1848 Revolution to the representatives of the democratic and petty-bourgeois republicans in the Constituent and Legislative Assemblies. This appellation was derived from the time of the Great French Revolution when the designation of the Mountain was applied to the Left wing in the Convention, who received this title because the benches on which Left Deputies were seated were situated high up in the Convention. The "Mountain" of 1848 which represented "the mass of the nation wavering between the bourgeoisie and the proletariat" (Marx) was only a pitiful parody of the "Mountain" of the period of the Great French Revolution. *Réforme* was the organ of the Mountain in 1848.

42. Concerning the historical basis which gave rise to Cavaignac in France, Lenin wrote as follows in his article entitled "The Class Origins of Present and 'Future' Cavaignacs":

"Let us recall the class role played by Cavaignac. In February 1848, the French monarchy was overthrown. The bourgeois republicans came into power. They, too, like our Cadets, wanted 'order,' meaning by that the restoration and the strengthening of the instruments for oppressing the masses developed by the monarchy: the police, the standing army, and the privileged bureaucracy. They, too, like our Cadets, wanted to put an end to the revolution, for they hated the revolutionary proletariat with its then very hazy 'social' (*i.e.*, Socialist) aspirations. They, too, like our Cadets, were implacably hostile to the idea of extending the French Revolution to the rest of Europe, the idea of changing it into a world proletarian revolution. They, too, like our Cadets, artfully utilized the petty-bourgeois 'Socialism' of Louis Blanc, by making him a member of the Cabinet and thus transforming him from a leader of the Socialist workers, which he wanted to be, into a mere appendage, hanger-on of the bourgeoisie.

"Such were the class interests, the position and the policy of the ruling class.

"Another basic social power was the petty bourgeoisie, vacillating, frightened by the Red specter, carried away by the outcries against the 'Anarchists.' In its aspirations dreamily and loquaciously 'Socialistic,' gladly calling itself a 'Socialist democracy' (even this very name has now been adopted by the Socialist-Revolutionaries and the Mensheviks!), the petty bourgeoisie was afraid to entrust itself to the leadership of the revolutionary proletariat, failing to realize that this fear condemned it to entrusting itself to the bourgeoisie. For, while in a society with a keen class struggle between the bourgeoisie and the proletariat, particularly when this struggle is inevitably made more acute by a revolution, there can be no 'middle' course, the whole essence of the class position and aspirations of the petty bourgeoisie consists in wanting the impossible, in aspiring towards the impossible, *i.e.*, towards just such a 'middle course.'

"The third determining class force was the proletariat which aspired, not towards a 'conciliation' with the bourgeoisie, but towards a victory over it, towards a fearless development of the revolution onward, and, what is more, on an international scale.

"This was the objective historical soil from which sprang Cavaignac. The vacillations of the petty bourgeoisie 'pushed it aside' from active roles, and the French Cadet, General Cavaignac, taking advantage of the fear of the petty bourgeoisie to entrust itself to the proletariat, decided to disarm the Paris workers, to shoot them down in large numbers.

"The revolution was terminated by this historical shooting; the petty bourgeoisie, numerically preponderant, had been and remained the politically impotent tail of the bourgeoisie, and three years later France again saw the restoration of a particularly vile form of Cæsarist monarchy." (Lenin, *Collected Works*, English edition, Vol. XX, Book II, pp. 255-56.)

43. The decrees of the Vienna Congress of the chief European powers (1814-15), which were of a purely reactionary character and attempted to restore the political order which existed up to the Great French Revolution and Napoleon I and which reduced the frontiers of France to those of 1792.

44. The device on the shield of the Bourbons.

45. Midas was the legendary king of the Phrygians. According to the old fable, at a musical competition between Apollo and Pan, Midas gave the preference to Pan. Because of this the indignant Apollo rewarded him by giving him ass's ears.

46. Soulouque was the name of the president of the Negro republic of Haiti, who in imitation of Napoleon I in 1850 proclaimed himself Emperor, surrounding himself with a whole staff of marshals and generals, establishing a court after the French model and in everything attempting to copy Napoleon. The masses of the people in France cleverly commented on the resemblance by dubbing Louis Bonaparte "Soulouque."

Toussaint L'Ouverture (1748-1803) was the Negro who headed the insurrection in San Domingo in 1796-1802. He was taken prisoner by the French forces and died in prison. The heroic struggle of Toussaint L'Ouverture is deeply enshrined in the memory of the Negroes in the U.S.A. and in the colonies, who see in him one of the first great leaders of the Negro struggle against imperialist exploitation and oppression.

47. Beaumarchais (1732-99). Pamphleteer and dramatist of the epoch before the French revolution, famous for his comedies *The Barber of Seville* and the *Marriage of Figaro*.

48. George Monk (1608-69) was an army general during the period of the English revolution which is associated with Cromwell. While engaged in carrying out the king's orders he was made prisoner by the revolutionary forces but after some years in prison he was liberated, and Cromwell gave him command first of a regiment and then of an army corps. Later Monk used the troops under him for the restoration of the old Stuart dynasty and the suppression of the revolution, for which he was liberally rewarded by Charles II.

49. Frightened by the threat of dissolution and by the military demonstration organized on January 29 by Louis Bonaparte, the Assembly had not the courage categorically to reject the proposal of Rateau and adopted a supplementary proposal, according to which the Assembly would be dissolved as

soon as it had issued laws on the State Council, the responsible president and his ministers and on the suffrage.

50. Fouquier-Tinville (1746-95) was one of the most eminent leaders of the Great French Revolution. When the Revolutionary Tribunal was organized on March 20, 1873, Fouquier-Tinville was appointed Public Prosecutor. In this capacity he conducted a merciless struggle against the enemies of the Revolution, applying the method of revolutionary terror.

51. The trial of those who had taken part in the events of May 1848, on the charge of conspiracy against the government. There appeared before the court, which was held in the town of Bourges, representatives of the proletariat (Blanqui, Barbès) and also part of the Mountain. Barbès, Albert, Flotte, Sobrier and Raspail were condemned to exile. The same sentence was passed in their absence on Louis Blanc, Caussidière, Lavisson and Hubert. Blanqui was sentenced to ten years' solitary imprisonment. In view of his illness it was considered that this term would be equivalent to a life sentence.

52. General Bréa, who was in command of part of the troops which suppressed the July rising of the Paris proletariat, was killed by the insurgents in Fontainebleau on June 25. In connection with this two of the participants in the rising were executed.

53. Louis Blanc and Caussidière were accused of complicity in the movement of May 15 and in the July rising of 1848 and handed over to the jurisdiction of the court. After the July days they both fled the country and the infuriated counter-revolution had to content itself with placarding their portraits on the pillory.

54. Haynau was an Austrian general, notorious for his ferocious punishment of the revolutionaries in the suppression of the revolution in Italy (1848) and in Hungary (1849). The "fame" of his cruelty and bloodthirstiness in the struggle against the revolution spread so far that, on the occasion of a visit to England, he was captured and flogged by the workers of a London factory.

55. Ems was the place of residence of Count Chambord (Henry V), Bourbon pretender to the French throne. His rival of the Orleans dynasty (Louis Philippe), who had fled to England after the February revolution, lived in Claremont near London. Thus Ems and Claremont were the centers of monarchist (royalist) intrigue.

56. The law was promulgated on December 13, 1899. On the basis of this law, teachers could be arbitrarily dismissed by the prefects and subjected to disciplinary investigation.

57. The decree on the organization of military command in the country was issued on February 15. The districts were divided into four areas which Marx compares with the areas ruled by Turkish pashas under governor-generals whose authority was marked by unrestricted supremacy of the military command.

58. The education law adopted by the National Assembly on March 16, 1850, put education entirely into the hands of the clergy and Jesuits.

59. Joseph Fouché (1763-1820). Active political figure in the Great French Revolution and afterwards in the First Empire. In the Convention he supported the Jacobins, later he participated in the counter-revolutionary action of the ninth Thermidor. After accumulating a considerable fortune by specu-

lation and abuse of his post, he took part in the coup of the Eighteenth Brumaire. In 1799 he was appointed Minister of Police. He kept this title with small interruptions until 1815, serving first the Republic, afterwards Napoleon I, then the Bourbons, later once more Napoleon, and finally for the second time Louis XVIII. Indispensable to all and ready to betray everyone, Fouché was one of the most expert and ambitious intriguers and careerists known to history.

60. On February 5, 1850, the Prefect of Police, Carlieu, a Bonapartist, ordered all "trees of liberty" to be cut down. The custom of planting "trees of liberty" in France is derived from the period of the Great French Revolution and was revived at the time of the July Revolution 1830 and of the February Revolution 1848. The "trees of liberty" were regarded as revolutionary emblems; demonstrations, dances, etc, were arranged in their vicinity and they were decorated with ribbons, inscriptions, etc.

61. On February 24th, the anniversary of the revolution, the people decorated the July column and the tombs of those who had fallen for freedom with flowers and wreaths. During the night the police removed the decorations, an act which evoked great dissatisfaction among the people.

62. The massacre of St. Bartholomew, on the night of August 23-24, 1572, one of the most bloody episodes in the history of religious struggles in France in the sixteenth century, when the protestant Huguenots were put to death by the order of the king.

63. Coblentz was a center of the counter-revolutionary émigrés at the time of the Great French Revolution.

64. Proudhon (1809-55) was not a Socialist. A typical representative of the petty property owners, he put forward in opposition to the system of capitalist property the system of petty commodity producers, who exchanged the products of their "labor" property according to the quantity of labor expended on them. This exchange was to be carried out by the People's Bank, projected by him, which would give out to the owners of goods special bonds serving as exchange tokens. The petty-bourgeois views of Proudhon were subjected to a crushing criticism by Marx in his *Poverty of Philosophy*.

65. Lamourette (1742-94), French prelate statesman, was a deputy in the Legislative Assembly during the Great French Revolution. He was famous for the so-called *baiser Lamourette*, a fraternal kiss by which he proposed to end all party dissension. Under the influence of his proposal, put forward with exceptional passion, on July 6, 1792, the representatives of the hostile parties embraced one another but, as might have been expected, on the following day this hypocritical "fraternal kiss" was forgotten.

66. The reference is to Louis Bonaparte's own organization built by him from the dregs of the society with whose aid he carried through his *coup d'état*. This organization was called the Society of December Tenth in memory of the day of election of Louis Bonaparte as President of the French Republic (December 10, 1848).